THE EXCITING WORLD OF CHURCHGOING

Dave Walker

CANTERBURY
PRESS
Norwich

First published in 2010 by the Canterbury Press Norwich
(a publishing imprint of Hymns Ancient & Modern Limited,
a registered charity)
13–17 Long Lane, London EC1A 9PN

www.canterburypress.co.uk

Second impression 2011

British Library Cataloguing in Publication data

A catalogue record for this book is available
from the British Library

ISBN 978 1 84825 029 1

Printed in the UK by
CPI Antony Rowe, Chippenham, Wiltshire

INTRODUCTION

Nobody starts to read a book of cartoons by looking at the introduction. According to some research I have carried out (observation of two or three people) I can report that most of the population begin such a book two thirds of the way through, and then work their way backwards towards the start. I hope therefore, that you've enjoyed the cartoons you've read thus far, and that you will enjoy the remaining third at some point.

In other research, academics have found that a large proportion of my books end up in the smallest rooms in Vicarages around the world. An edition in which every fifth page is marked with the phrase 'Not to be removed from the Vicarage toilet' is currently being considered by the publishers.

Thanks must go to the various people who have helped me. The main one is my wife, Charlotte, who in fact thinks up most of the ideas, the rest being sent in by helpful members of the public. Their combined efforts allow me to keep up the appearance of having one good idea a week. Please continue to send me information on subjects that you think deserve wider coverage to dave@cartoonchurch.com.

At this point I face the quandary faced by many writers of post-birthday thank you letters – whether to stick to the point or address sundry matters of interest. I must do the former, and direct interested readers to my blog, www.cartoonchurch.com/blog, where engaging topics such as my recent studio move to the heart of industrial Basildon are analysed in some detail.

I hope that this body of work contributes to our collective understanding of the Church, and means that we can all make a little more sense of it. In future years we may remember 2010 as the year when there was a small blip in the national church rota membership statistics, as readers of this volume decided they'd like to get more involved, but then, after a few short weeks, changed their minds. Or we may not – it is too early to say at this stage.

Dave Walker
The heart of industrial Basildon.
May 2010

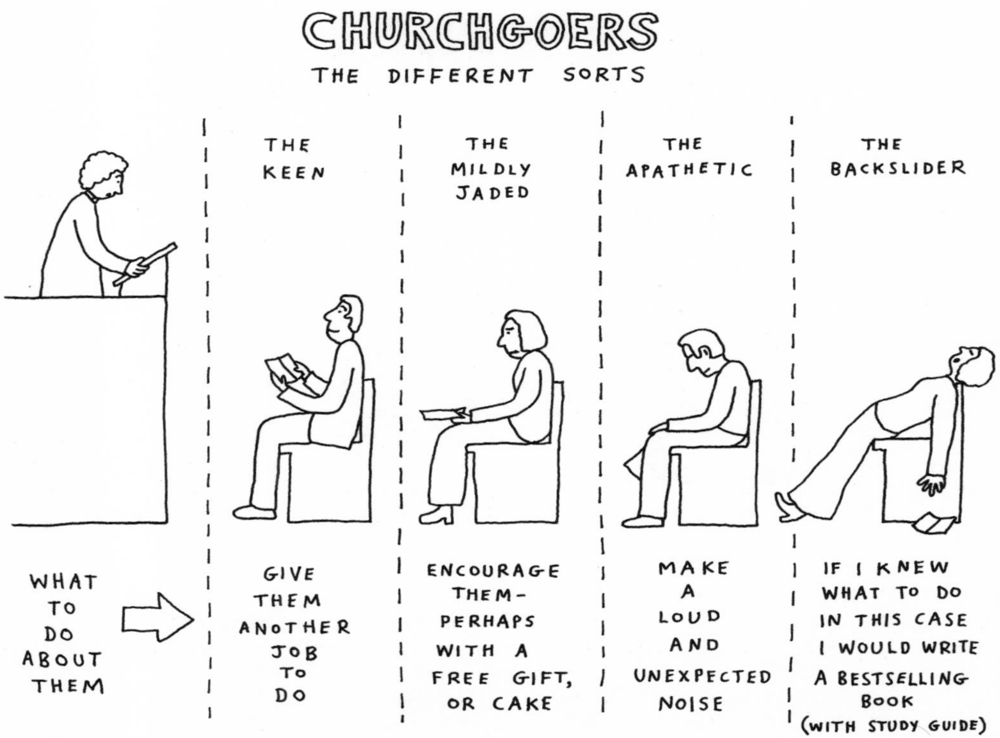
CHURCHGOERS
THE DIFFERENT SORTS
THE KEEN
THE MILDLY JADED
THE APATHETIC
THE BACKSLIDER
WHAT TO DO ABOUT THEM
GIVE THEM ANOTHER JOB TO DO
ENCOURAGE THEM- PERHAPS WITH A FREE GIFT, OR CAKE
MAKE A LOUD AND UNEXPECTED NOISE
IF I KNEW WHAT TO DO IN THIS CASE I WOULD WRITE A BESTSELLING BOOK (WITH STUDY GUIDE)

INFORMATION FOR VISITORS

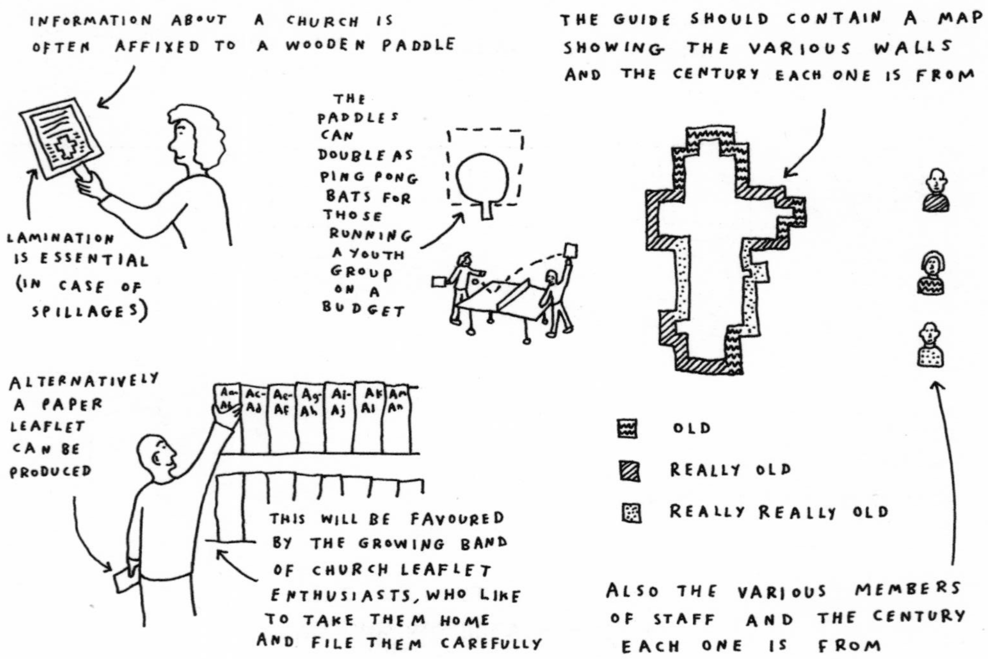
INFORMATION ABOUT A CHURCH IS OFTEN AFFIXED TO A WOODEN PADDLE
LAMINATION IS ESSENTIAL (IN CASE OF SPILLAGES)
THE PADDLES CAN DOUBLE AS PING PONG BATS FOR THOSE RUNNING A YOUTH GROUP ON A BUDGET
THE GUIDE SHOULD CONTAIN A MAP SHOWING THE VARIOUS WALLS AND THE CENTURY EACH ONE IS FROM
OLD
REALLY OLD
REALLY REALLY OLD
ALSO THE VARIOUS MEMBERS OF STAFF AND THE CENTURY EACH ONE IS FROM
ALTERNATIVELY A PAPER LEAFLET CAN BE PRODUCED
THIS WILL BE FAVOURED BY THE GROWING BAND OF CHURCH LEAFLET ENTHUSIASTS, WHO LIKE TO TAKE THEM HOME AND FILE THEM CAREFULLY

PUNCTUALITY

BEATING THE CROWDS

HOW TO MAKE SURE YOU GET A SEAT IN THE SUNDAY SERVICE

SELECT YOUR PEW

BUY TICKETS WELL IN ADVANCE
(THESE DAYS YOU CAN DO THIS KIND OF THING USING COMPUTERS)

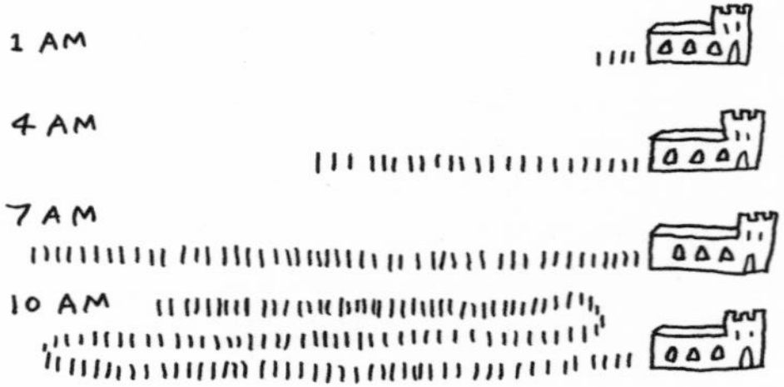
1 AM
4 AM
7 AM
10 AM

JOIN THE QUEUE EARLY

JOIN THE THOUSANDS OF PEOPLE ACROSS THE COUNTRY WHO DO A JOB IN CHURCH JUST TO GET A GOOD SEAT

SO... DAVID

REMEMBER: IT IS WHO YOU KNOW. GET ON FIRST NAME TERMS WITH A MEMBER OF THE CLERGY

VOLUNTEER TRANSPORT

THIS IS FOR MEMBERS OF THE CONGREGATION WHO CANNOT GET TO CHURCH BY OTHER MEANS. A ROUTE IS PLANNED TO TAKE ACCOUNT OF THEIR SPECIAL REQUIREMENTS

MR WILLIAMS

MUST HAVE A WINDOW SEAT. LIKES TO SPEND A MINUTE OR SO GREETING EVERY OTHER OCCUPANT

MRS SMITH

MUST BE PICKED UP FIRST AND SIT IN THE FRONT. DOESN'T GET ON WITH MRS DAVIES OR MR TAYLOR

MRS DAVIES

NEEDS THE TOILET EVERY TEN MINUTES. CAN'T ABIDE THE RADIO BEING ON

MRS THOMAS

REQUIRES A 'TEN MINUTE WARNING' TELEPHONE CALL BEFORE PICKUP. MUST SIT NEXT TO MRS WILSON

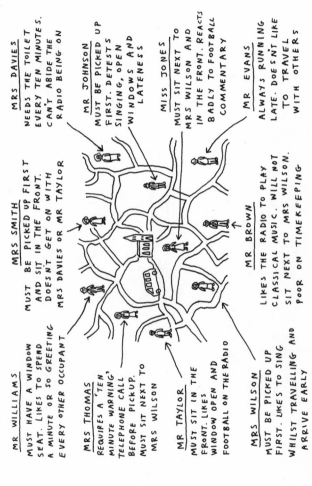

MR JOHNSON

MUST BE PICKED UP FIRST. DETESTS SINGING, OPEN WINDOWS AND LATENESS

MR TAYLOR

MUST SIT IN THE FRONT. LIKES WINDOW OPEN AND FOOTBALL ON THE RADIO

MISS JONES

MUST SIT NEXT TO MRS WILSON AND IN THE FRONT. REACTS BADLY TO FOOTBALL COMMENTARY

MRS WILSON

MUST BE PICKED UP FIRST. LIKES TO SING WHILST TRAVELLING AND ARRIVE EARLY

MR BROWN

LIKES THE RADIO TO PLAY CLASSICAL MUSIC. WILL NOT SIT NEXT TO MRS WILSON. POOR ON TIMEKEEPING

MR EVANS

ALWAYS RUNNING LATE. DOESN'T LIKE TO TRAVEL WITH OTHERS

BEFORE THE SERVICE

THE CONGREGATION UNDERTAKE CAREFUL DEVOTIONAL PREPARATION FOR WORSHIP

HALF OF THEM DISRUPT THE PRE-SERVICE QUIETNESS WITH THEIR CONTINUAL WHISPERING
THE OTHER HALF SEEK TO SILENCE THEM THROUGH THE MEDIUM OF FROWNING

IN THE VESTRY

THE FINAL MOMENTS BEFORE THE SERVICE

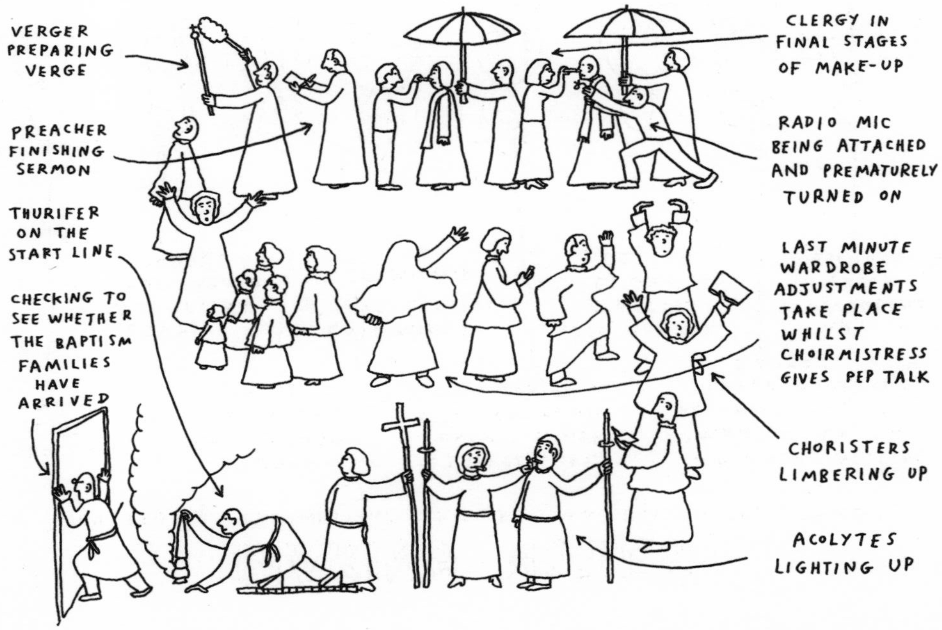
VERGER PREPARING VERGE
PREACHER FINISHING SERMON
THURIFER ON THE START LINE
CHECKING TO SEE WHETHER THE BAPTISM FAMILIES HAVE ARRIVED
CLERGY IN FINAL STAGES OF MAKE-UP
RADIO MIC BEING ATTACHED AND PREMATURELY TURNED ON
LAST MINUTE WARDROBE ADJUSTMENTS TAKE PLACE WHILST CHOIRMISTRESS GIVES PEP TALK
CHORISTERS LIMBERING UP
ACOLYTES LIGHTING UP

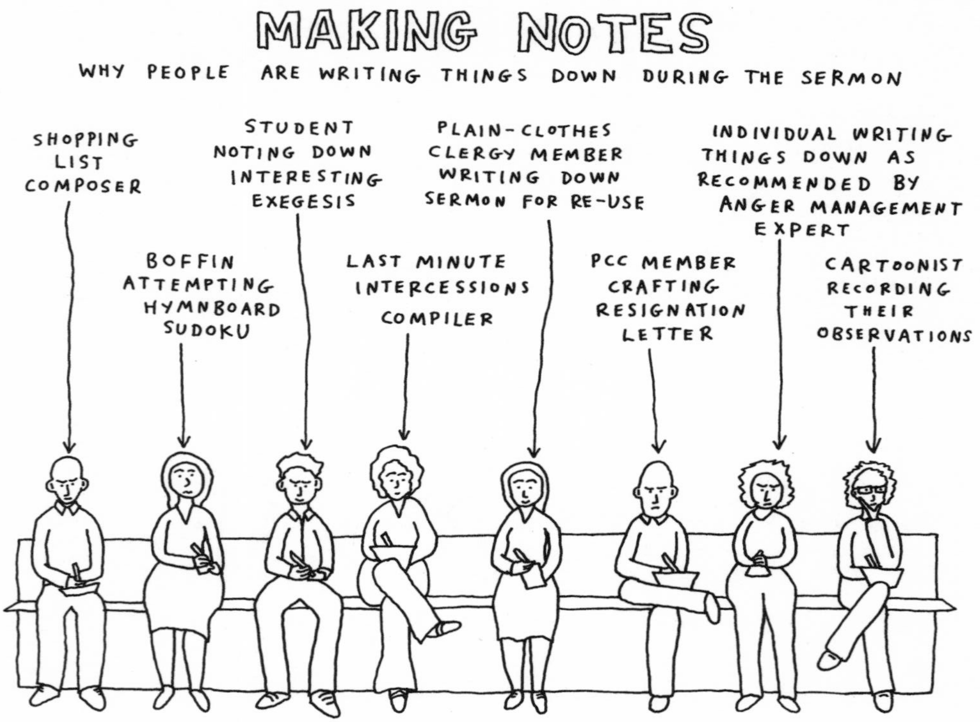
MAKING NOTES
WHY PEOPLE ARE WRITING THINGS DOWN DURING THE SERMON
SHOPPING LIST COMPOSER
BOFFIN ATTEMPTING HYMNBOARD SUDOKU
STUDENT NOTING DOWN INTERESTING EXEGESIS
LAST MINUTE INTERCESSIONS COMPILER
PLAIN-CLOTHES CLERGY MEMBER WRITING DOWN SERMON FOR RE-USE
PCC MEMBER CRAFTING RESIGNATION LETTER
INDIVIDUAL WRITING THINGS DOWN AS RECOMMENDED BY ANGER MANAGEMENT EXPERT
CARTOONIST RECORDING THEIR OBSERVATIONS

COFFEE CUPS

WE DEMONSTRATE OUR UNITY THROUGH THE SHARING OF A COMMUNAL AFTER-SERVICE COFFEE CUP

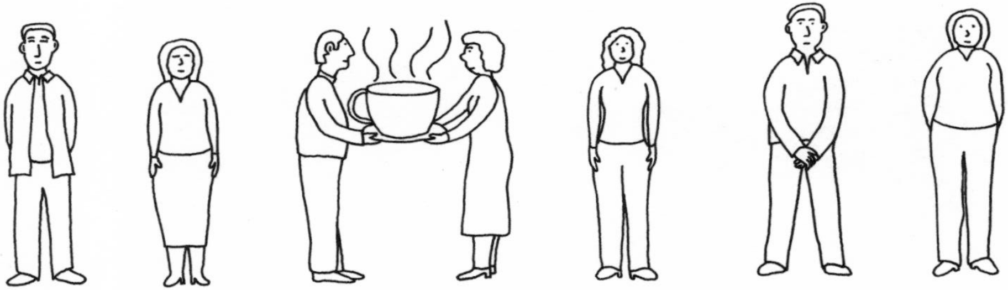

IT IS RUMOURED THAT IN SOME CHURCHES EACH PERSON HAS THEIR OWN INDIVIDUAL COFFEE CUP (WE SECRETLY REGARD THIS AS A BIT ODD)

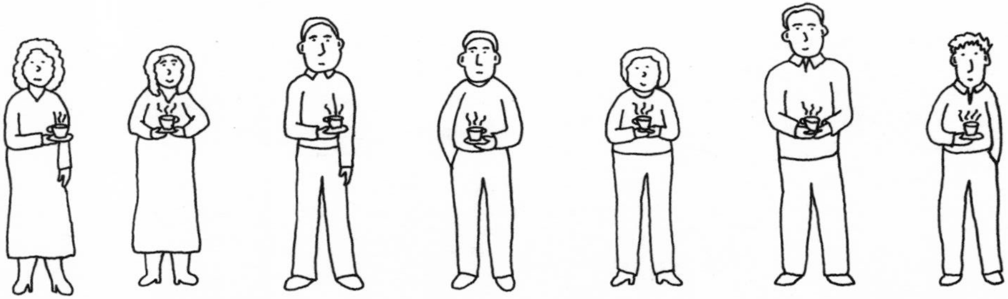

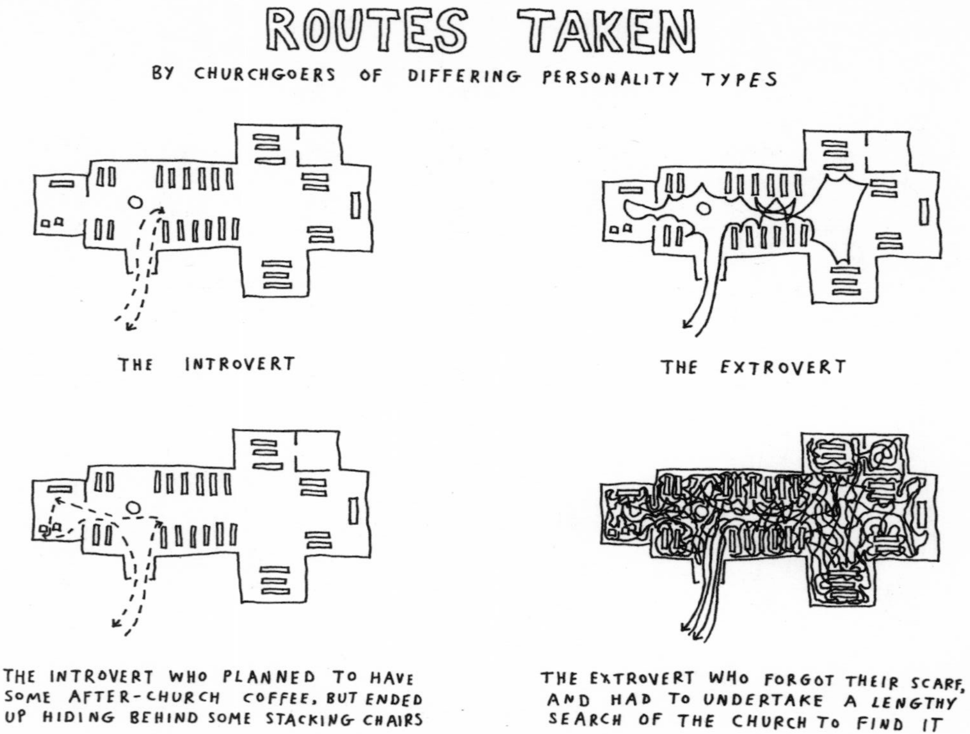
ROUTES TAKEN
BY CHURCHGOERS OF DIFFERING PERSONALITY TYPES
THE INTROVERT
THE EXTROVERT
THE INTROVERT WHO PLANNED TO HAVE SOME AFTER-CHURCH COFFEE, BUT ENDED UP HIDING BEHIND SOME STACKING CHAIRS
THE EXTROVERT WHO FORGOT THEIR SCARF, AND HAD TO UNDERTAKE A LENGTHY SEARCH OF THE CHURCH TO FIND IT

PROBLEMS

WHAT TO DO IF YOU HAVE ONE WHILST IN CHURCH

① SUMMON A SIDESPERSON. THEY HAVE FULL ACCESS TO A WIDE RANGE OF HYMN BOOKS AND OTHER SERVICE MATERIAL – THEY WILL BE ABLE TO ASSIST IN 95% OF CASES

② IF MORE SPECIALIST HELP IS REQUIRED A CHURCHWARDEN OR MEMBER OF THE CLERGY SHOULD BE SOUGHT. BOTH CARRY LARGE BUNCHES OF KEYS THAT UNLOCK ALL SORTS OF THINGS

③ IN THE HIGHLY UNLIKELY EVENT THAT YOU ARE UNABLE TO FIND HELP LOCALLY YOU CAN CONSULT A BISHOP. THEY HAVE GREAT EXPERIENCE AND QUITE A LOT OF BOOKS

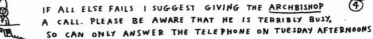

④ IF ALL ELSE FAILS I SUGGEST GIVING THE ARCHBISHOP A CALL. PLEASE BE AWARE THAT HE IS TERRIBLY BUSY, SO CAN ONLY ANSWER THE TELEPHONE ON TUESDAY AFTERNOONS

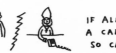

NUMBERS

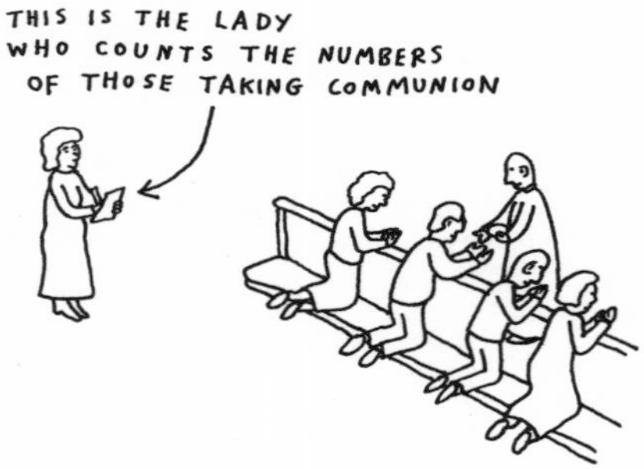
THIS IS THE LADY
WHO COUNTS THE NUMBERS
OF THOSE TAKING COMMUNION

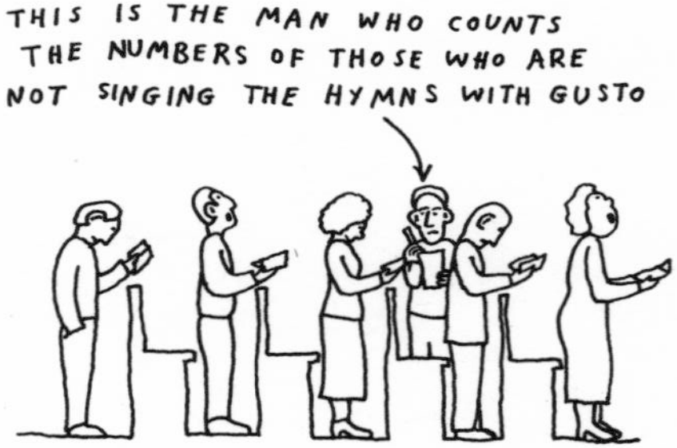
THIS IS THE MAN WHO COUNTS
THE NUMBERS OF THOSE WHO ARE
NOT SINGING THE HYMNS WITH GUSTO

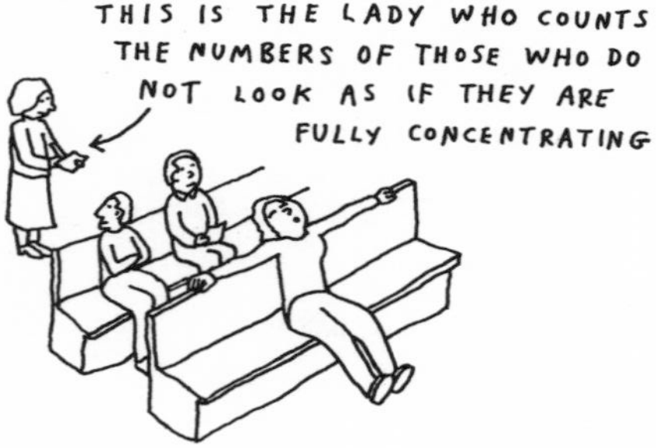
THIS IS THE LADY WHO COUNTS
THE NUMBERS OF THOSE WHO DO
NOT LOOK AS IF THEY ARE
FULLY CONCENTRATING

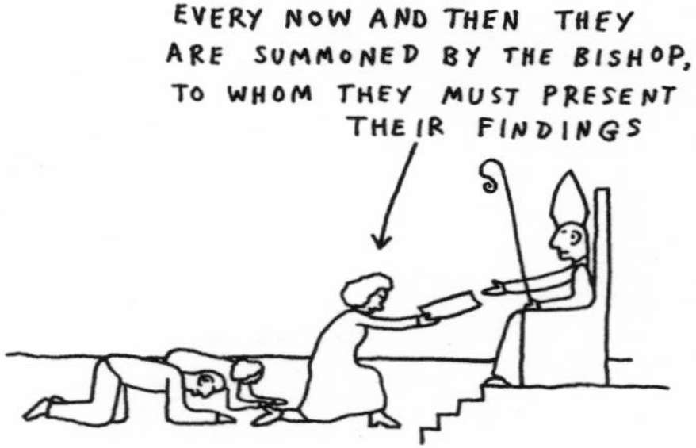
EVERY NOW AND THEN THEY
ARE SUMMONED BY THE BISHOP,
TO WHOM THEY MUST PRESENT
THEIR FINDINGS

THE BAPTISMAL PARTY
THE BAPTISMAL PARTY
THE REGULAR CONGREGATION
DRESSED SMARTLY
DRESSED SCRUFFILY
POPULAR MUSIC RING TONES
SACRED MUSIC RING TONES
HYMNS
INDIVIDUAL LEAVING FOR A CIGARETTE BREAK
INDIVIDUAL LEAVING TO UNDERTAKE A WORTHY TASK OF SOME SORT
CAN WE GO HOME NOW?
INAPPROPRIATE CINEMATOGRAPHY
INAPPROPRIATE COMMENTS
DO NOT REALLY KNOW WHAT IS GOING ON
DO NOT REALLY KNOW WHAT IS GOING ON

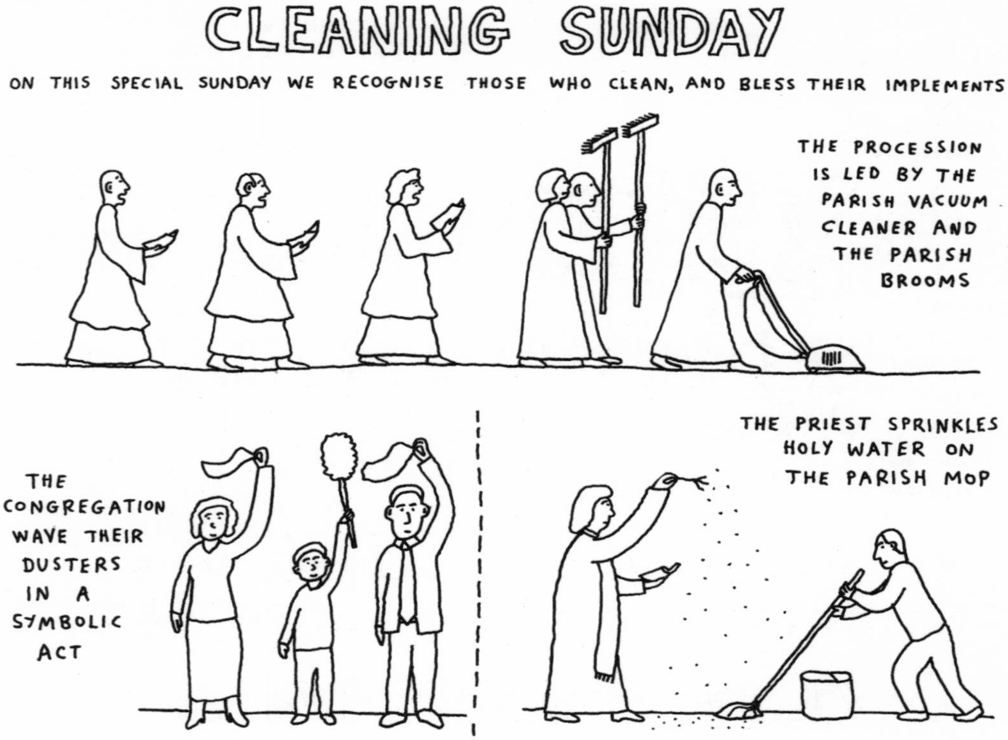
CLEANING SUNDAY
ON THIS SPECIAL SUNDAY WE RECOGNISE THOSE WHO CLEAN, AND BLESS THEIR IMPLEMENTS
THE PROCESSION IS LED BY THE PARISH VACUUM CLEANER AND THE PARISH BROOMS
THE CONGREGATION WAVE THEIR DUSTERS IN A SYMBOLIC ACT
THE PRIEST SPRINKLES HOLY WATER ON THE PARISH MOP

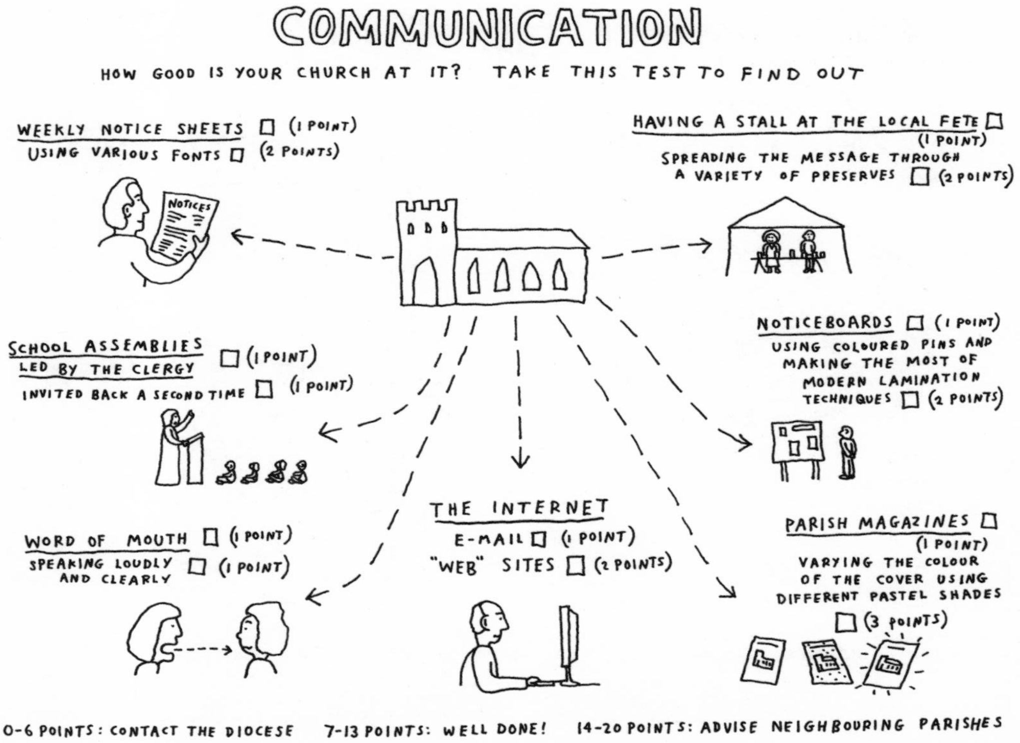
COMMUNICATION
HOW GOOD IS YOUR CHURCH AT IT? TAKE THIS TEST TO FIND OUT
WEEKLY NOTICE SHEETS ☐ (1 POINT)
USING VARIOUS FONTS ☐ (2 POINTS)
NOTICES
HAVING A STALL AT THE LOCAL FETE ☐ (1 POINT)
SPREADING THE MESSAGE THROUGH A VARIETY OF PRESERVES ☐ (2 POINTS)
SCHOOL ASSEMBLIES LED BY THE CLERGY ☐ (1 POINT)
INVITED BACK A SECOND TIME ☐ (1 POINT)
NOTICEBOARDS ☐ (1 POINT)
USING COLOURED PINS AND MAKING THE MOST OF MODERN LAMINATION TECHNIQUES ☐ (2 POINTS)
THE INTERNET
E-MAIL ☐ (1 POINT)
"WEB" SITES ☐ (2 POINTS)
WORD OF MOUTH ☐ (1 POINT)
SPEAKING LOUDLY AND CLEARLY ☐ (1 POINT)
PARISH MAGAZINES ☐ (1 POINT)
VARYING THE COLOUR OF THE COVER USING DIFFERENT PASTEL SHADES ☐ (3 POINTS)
0-6 POINTS: CONTACT THE DIOCESE
7-13 POINTS: WELL DONE!
14-20 POINTS: ADVISE NEIGHBOURING PARISHES

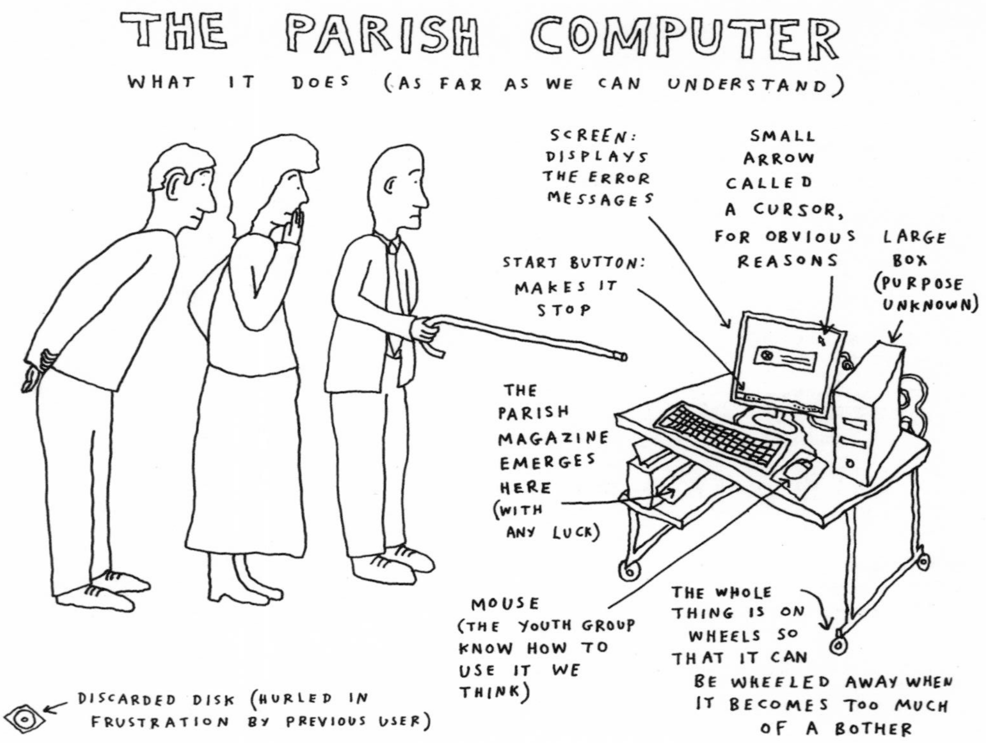
THE PARISH COMPUTER
WHAT IT DOES (AS FAR AS WE CAN UNDERSTAND)
SCREEN: DISPLAYS THE ERROR MESSAGES
SMALL ARROW CALLED A CURSOR, FOR OBVIOUS REASONS
LARGE BOX (PURPOSE UNKNOWN)
START BUTTON: MAKES IT STOP
THE PARISH MAGAZINE EMERGES HERE (WITH ANY LUCK)
MOUSE (THE YOUTH GROUP KNOW HOW TO USE IT WE THINK)
THE WHOLE THING IS ON WHEELS SO THAT IT CAN BE WHEELED AWAY WHEN IT BECOMES TOO MUCH OF A BOTHER
DISCARDED DISK (HURLED IN FRUSTRATION BY PREVIOUS USER)

PARISH LIFE

BEFORE THE INVENTION OF THE COMPUTER

FREE DESK SPACE WHICH FUTURE GENERATIONS WOULD USE FOR PRINTERS, SCANNERS, ETC, ETC

THE NOTICE SHEET
WAS COPIED BY HAND

MESSAGES WERE DELIVERED
ON FOOT

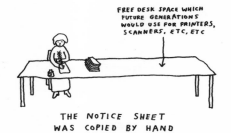

A GREAT BIG BELL WAS RUNG
TO TELL PEOPLE THINGS

PEOPLE HAD HOBBIES, AND DRANK
AFTERNOON TEA, AND DID NOT SPEND
EVERY SPARE HOUR OF THE DAY
IN AN EXASPERATED STATE TRYING
TO MAKE THE WRETCHED THING WORK

THE INTERNET
HOW IT BRINGS US TOGETHER
I FEEL IN THE MOOD FOR A STUPID AND POINTLESS ARGUMENT IN AN ONLINE FORUM TODAY
I FEEL IN THE MOOD FOR A POINTLESS AND STUPID ARGUMENT IN AN ONLINE FORUM TODAY

THE DATA PROJECTOR

HOW TO UNDERSTAND THE ERROR MESSAGES

A CONNECTION TO THE SERVER COULD NOT BE ESTABLISHED

THEY HAVE WANDERED OFF AND ARE CONVERSING WITH ONE OF THE ACOLYTES

WARNING: NOT ENOUGH RESOURCES

THE TREASURER NEEDS TO HAVE ONE OF HIS 'SPECIAL CHATS'

NOT RESPONDING

PERHAPS THERE IS A PROBLEM WITH THE RADIO MICROPHONE

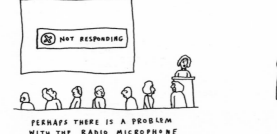

YOU HAVE PERFORMED AN ILLEGAL OPERATION

IT IS NOT PERMISSIBLE TO CONDUCT THAT SORT OF BLESSING

HYMN BOOKS V DATA PROJECTORS

THE PROS AND CONS

THE ADVANTAGES OF HYMN BOOKS

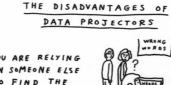

SOMETHING TO LOOK AT DURING IDLE MOMENTS

PICKING UP AND PUTTING DOWN A BOOK IS GOOD FOR FITNESS

YOU CAN SEE HOW MANY VERSES YOU STILL HAVE TO GET THROUGH

THE DISADVANTAGES OF DATA PROJECTORS

YOU ARE RELYING ON SOMEONE ELSE TO FIND THE CORRECT VERSE

HANDS ARE FREE, SO THERE IS A TEMPTATION TO SCRATCH OR FIDDLE

THERE IS A RISK THAT OPERATORS WILL USE INAPPROPRIATE BACKGROUNDS

THIS ANALYSIS WOULD SEEM TO SUGGEST THAT HYMN BOOKS ARE BETTER

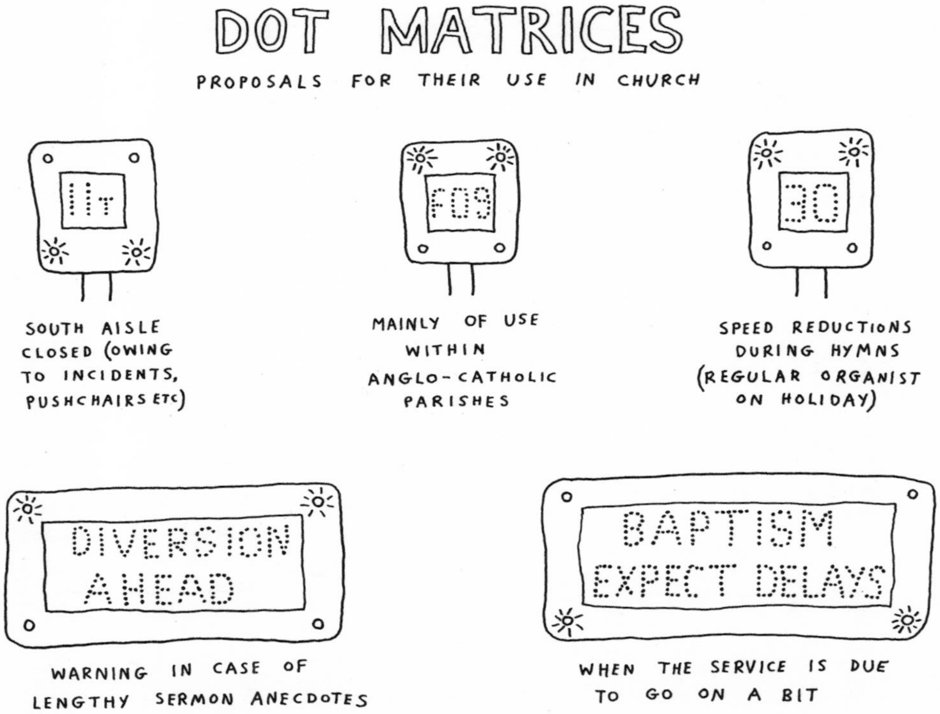
DOT MATRICES
PROPOSALS FOR THEIR USE IN CHURCH
SOUTH AISLE CLOSED (OWING TO INCIDENTS, PUSHCHAIRS ETC)
F09
MAINLY OF USE WITHIN ANGLO-CATHOLIC PARISHES
30
SPEED REDUCTIONS DURING HYMNS (REGULAR ORGANIST ON HOLIDAY)
DIVERSION AHEAD
WARNING IN CASE OF LENGTHY SERMON ANECDOTES
BAPTISM EXPECT DELAYS
WHEN THE SERVICE IS DUE TO GO ON A BIT

THE SOUND DESK OPERATOR
RESPONSIBILITIES
MOVING THE SLIDER UP A BIT
MOVING THE SLIDER DOWN A BIT
MOVING THE SLIDER BACK UP A BIT
EVERY NOW AND THEN PRESSING THE 'SUDDEN UNEXPECTED FEEDBACK' BUTTON
PERKS OF THE JOB
BEING ABLE TO HAVE MINTS DURING THE SERMON
HAVING SOLE RESPONSIBILITY FOR THE 'WIRES AND CABLES' BOX

THE P.C.C.

ONE OF THEIR JOBS IS TO HELP THE VICAR SPEND THE CHURCH FUNDS

THE P.C.C.

HOW TO ENCOURAGE BONDING

WHITE WATER BUNGEE PAINTBALLING

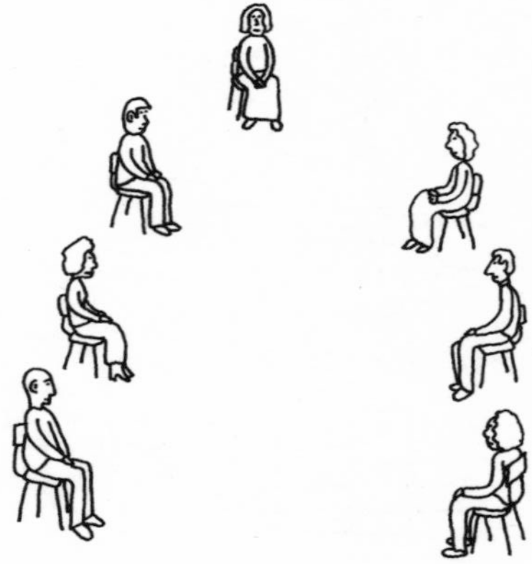

GOING ON A RETREAT

ELECTIONS

THESE ARE OFTEN HELD AT THIS TIME OF YEAR.
VOTES ARE CANVASSED BY THE FOLLOWING MEANS:

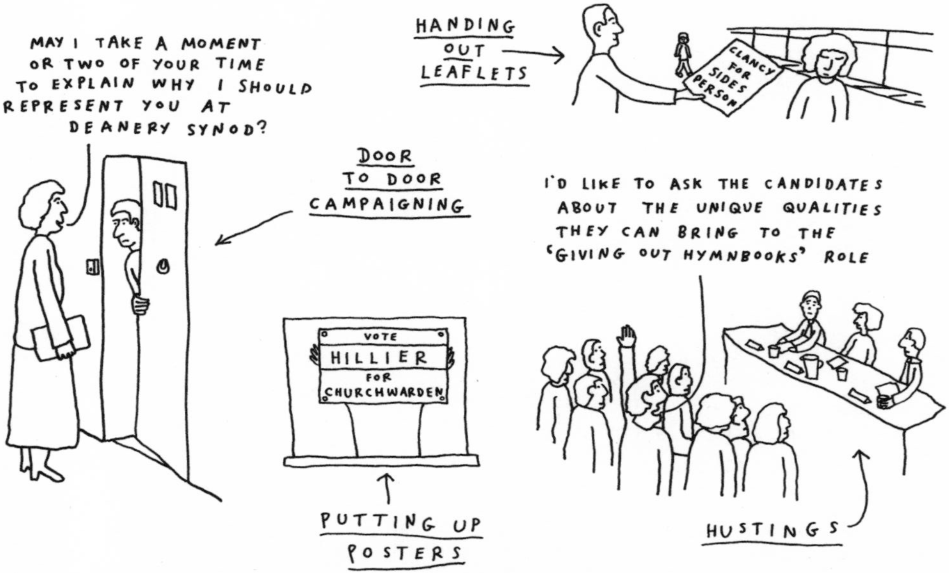
MAY I TAKE A MOMENT OR TWO OF YOUR TIME TO EXPLAIN WHY I SHOULD REPRESENT YOU AT DEANERY SYNOD?
DOOR TO DOOR CAMPAIGNING
HANDING OUT LEAFLETS
CLANCY FOR SIDES PERSON
VOTE HILLIER FOR CHURCHWARDEN
PUTTING UP POSTERS
I'D LIKE TO ASK THE CANDIDATES ABOUT THE UNIQUE QUALITIES THEY CAN BRING TO THE 'GIVING OUT HYMNBOOKS' ROLE
HUSTINGS

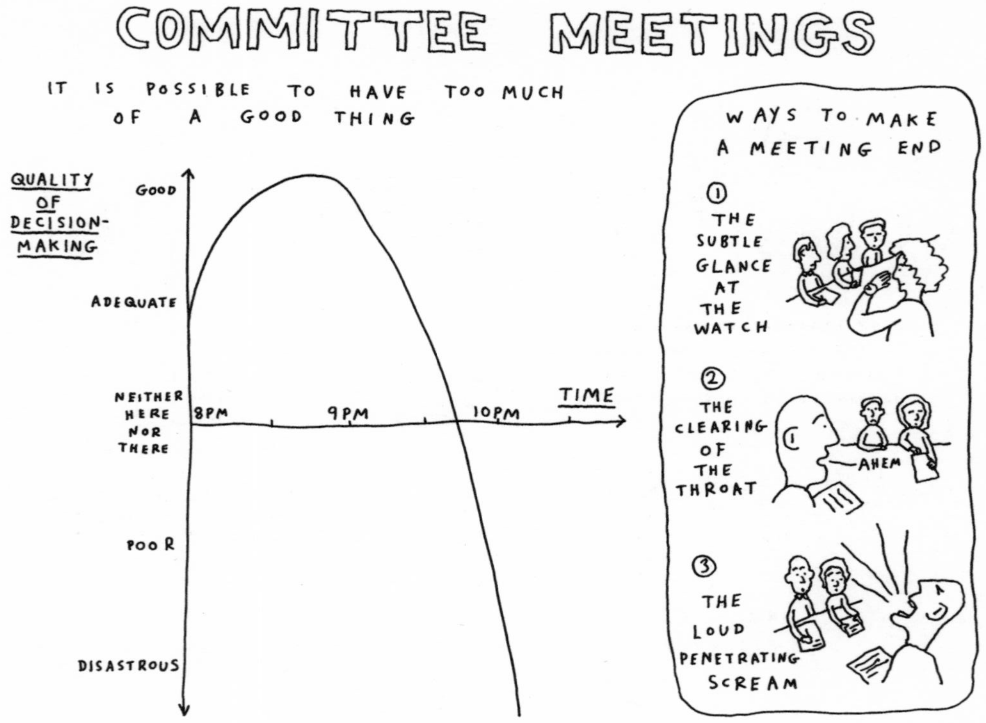
COMMITTEE MEETINGS
IT IS POSSIBLE TO HAVE TOO MUCH OF A GOOD THING
QUALITY OF DECISION-MAKING
GOOD
ADEQUATE
NEITHER HERE NOR THERE
POOR
DISASTROUS
8PM
9PM
10PM
TIME
WAYS TO MAKE A MEETING END
① THE SUBTLE GLANCE AT THE WATCH
② THE CLEARING OF THE THROAT
AHEM
③ THE LOUD PENETRATING SCREAM

THE SOCIAL COMMITTEE

THEY MEET TO TRY TO THINK OF A PROGRAMME OF ENJOYABLE ACTIVITIES

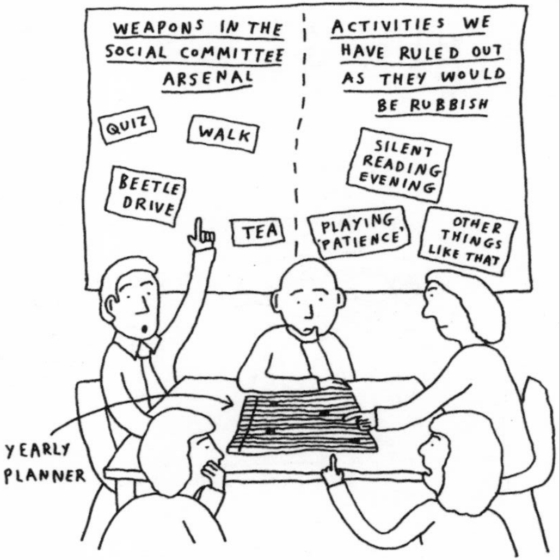
WEAPONS IN THE SOCIAL COMMITTEE ARSENAL
QUIZ
WALK
BEETLE DRIVE
TEA
ACTIVITIES WE HAVE RULED OUT AS THEY WOULD BE RUBBISH
SILENT READING EVENING
PLAYING 'PATIENCE'
OTHER THINGS LIKE THAT
YEARLY PLANNER

IT IS IMPORTANT THAT THE ACTIVITIES ARE EVENLY SPREAD THROUGHOUT THE YEAR TO AVOID SEASONS OF OVEREXCITEMENT

THE SOCIAL COMMITTEE IS MADE UP OF CATERING EXPERTS AND THOSE WHO WERE IN THE WRONG PLACE AT THE WRONG TIME

DIAGRAM SHOWING HOW SOMEONE CAN BE CAUGHT IN THE WRONG PLACE AT THE WRONG TIME

(VIEWED FROM ABOVE)

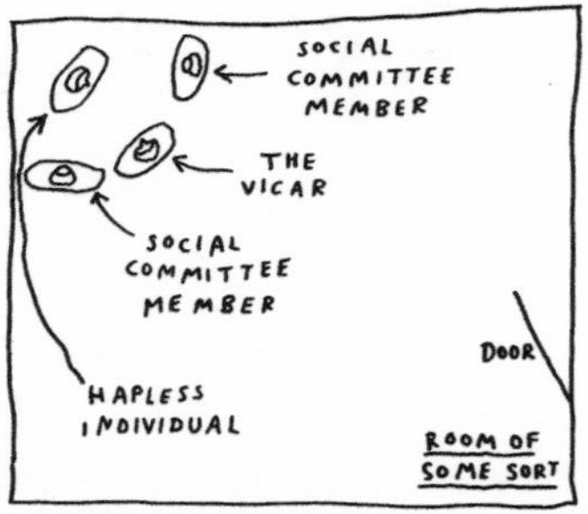
SOCIAL COMMITTEE MEMBER
THE VICAR
SOCIAL COMMITTEE MEMBER
HAPLESS INDIVIDUAL
DOOR
ROOM OF SOME SORT

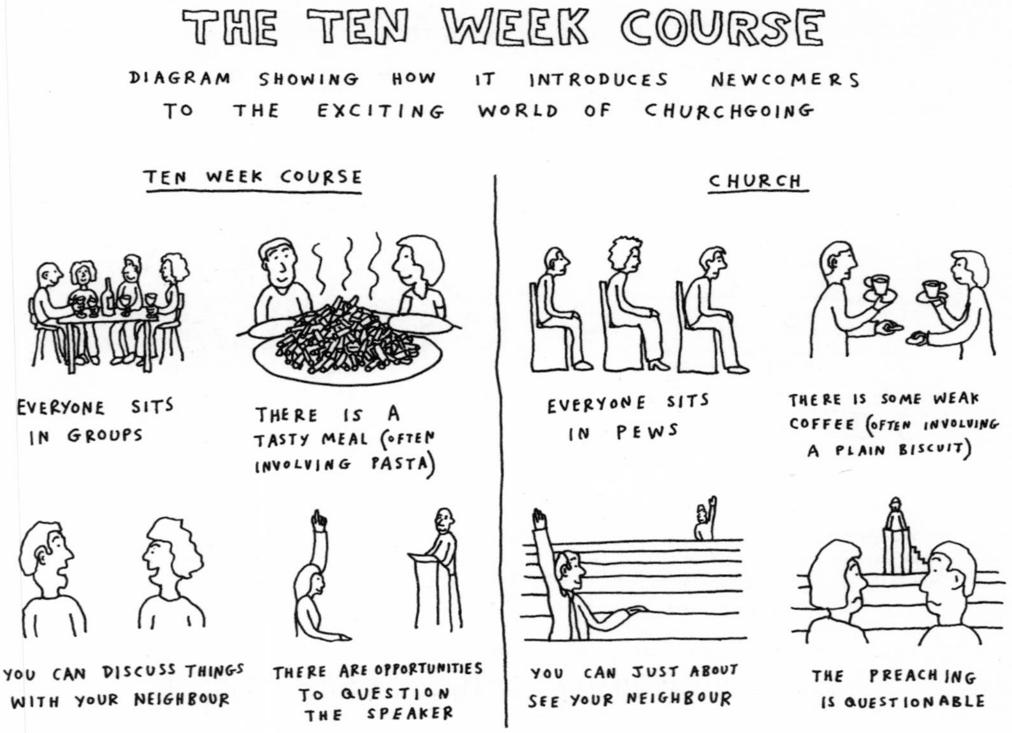

THE TEN WEEK COURSE

DIAGRAM SHOWING HOW IT INTRODUCES NEWCOMERS
TO THE EXCITING WORLD OF CHURCHGOING

TEN WEEK COURSE

EVERYONE SITS
IN GROUPS

THERE IS A
TASTY MEAL (OFTEN
INVOLVING PASTA)

YOU CAN DISCUSS THINGS
WITH YOUR NEIGHBOUR

THERE ARE OPPORTUNITIES
TO QUESTION
THE SPEAKER

CHURCH

EVERYONE SITS
IN PEWS

THERE IS SOME WEAK
COFFEE (OFTEN INVOLVING
A PLAIN BISCUIT)

YOU CAN JUST ABOUT
SEE YOUR NEIGHBOUR

THE PREACHING
IS QUESTIONABLE

SEGREGATION

THE LADIES' GROUP

THEY HAVE SPEAKERS WHO TALK ABOUT:

- KNITTING PATTERNS
- HANDBAG ESSENTIALS
- MAKING PRETTY THINGS WITH BITS OF RIBBON

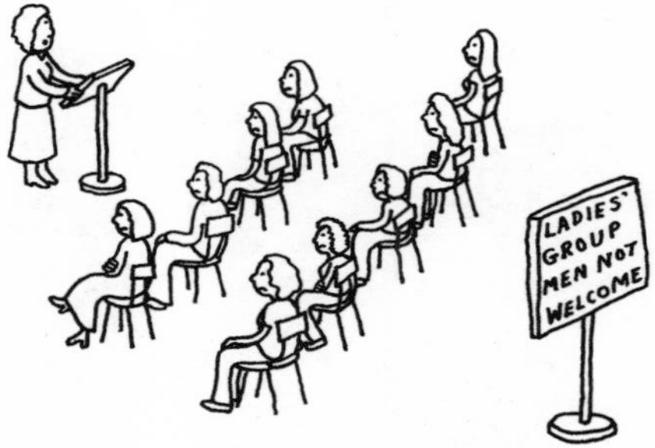

BUT SECRETLY THEY WOULD LIKE TO LEARN ABOUT:

- LAWNMOWER MAINTENANCE
- CHOPPING UP LOGS
- WOLF WHISTLING

THE MEN'S GROUP

THEY HAVE SPEAKERS WHO TALK ABOUT:

- LAWNMOWER MAINTENANCE
- CHOPPING UP LOGS
- WOLF WHISTLING

BUT SECRETLY THEY WOULD LIKE TO LEARN ABOUT:

- KNITTING PATTERNS
- HANDBAG ESSENTIALS
- MAKING PRETTY THINGS WITH BITS OF RIBBON

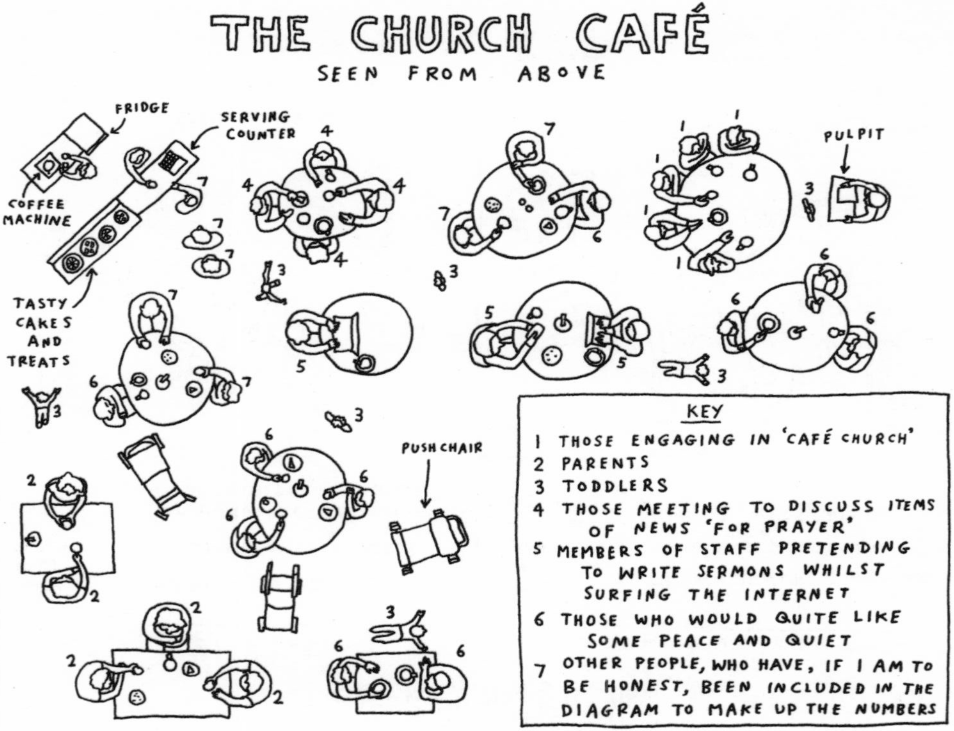
THE CHURCH CAFÉ
SEEN FROM ABOVE
FRIDGE
SERVING COUNTER
COFFEE MACHINE
TASTY CAKES AND TREATS
PULPIT
PUSHCHAIR
KEY
1 THOSE ENGAGING IN 'CAFÉ CHURCH'
2 PARENTS
3 TODDLERS
4 THOSE MEETING TO DISCUSS ITEMS OF NEWS 'FOR PRAYER'
5 MEMBERS OF STAFF PRETENDING TO WRITE SERMONS WHILST SURFING THE INTERNET
6 THOSE WHO WOULD QUITE LIKE SOME PEACE AND QUIET
7 OTHER PEOPLE, WHO HAVE, IF I AM TO BE HONEST, BEEN INCLUDED IN THE DIAGRAM TO MAKE UP THE NUMBERS

ROTAS

WHAT HAPPENS WHEN THEY GO WRONG

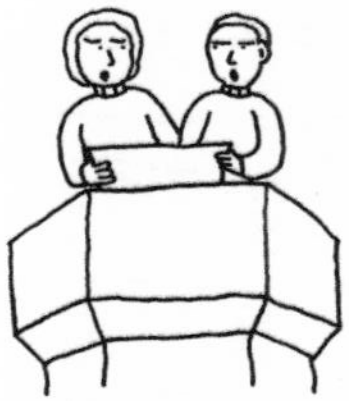

WHEN TWO PREACHERS BOTH THINK IT IS THEIR WEEK

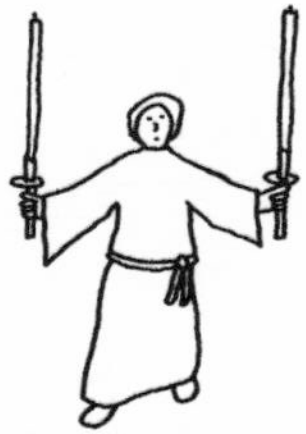

WHEN ONLY ONE ACOLYTE SHOWS UP

WHEN TWO RIVAL HOME GROUPS BOTH THINK IT IS THEIR TURN TO BE ON COFFEE DUTY

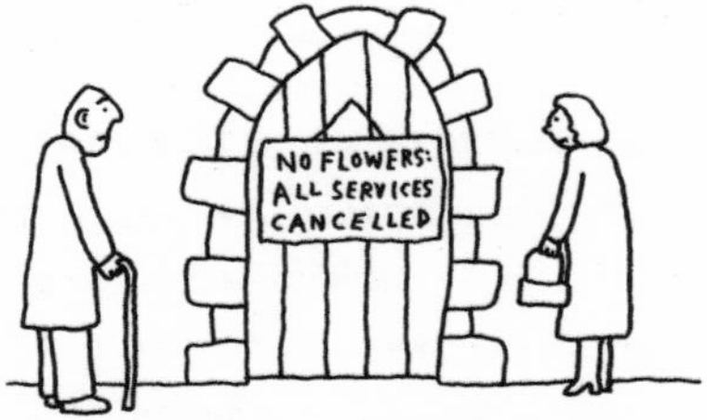
NO FLOWERS: ALL SERVICES CANCELLED

WHEN A DRAWING PIN FAILS, CAUSING THE FLOWER ROTA TO FALL BEHIND A RADIATOR

CHANGING THE TEATOWELS

ACCORDING TO LEGEND THERE IS A LADY WHO CHANGES THE TEATOWELS IN THE CHURCH KITCHEN FROM TIME TO TIME.

NOONE CAN REMEMBER SEEING HER – THE ONLY EVIDENCE IS THESE FADED PHOTOGRAPHS, HANDED DOWN FROM GENERATION TO GENERATION

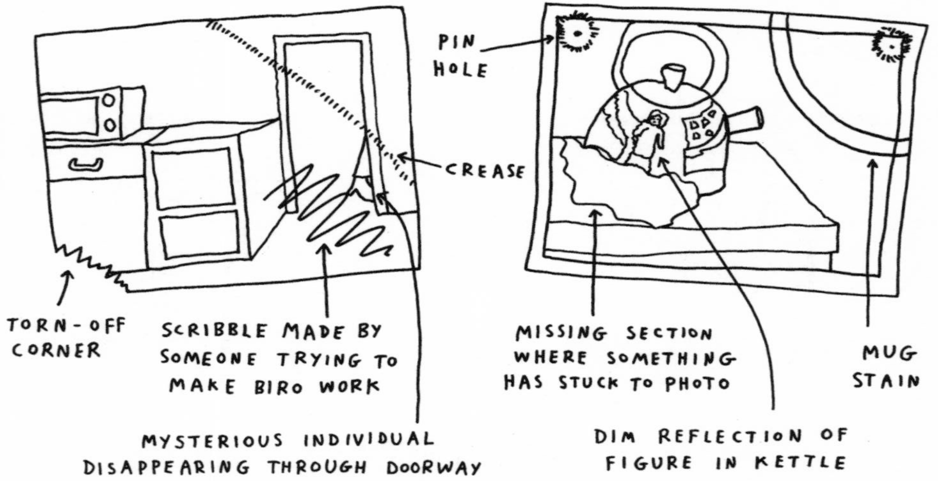
PIN HOLE
CREASE
TORN-OFF CORNER
SCRIBBLE MADE BY SOMEONE TRYING TO MAKE BIRO WORK
MYSTERIOUS INDIVIDUAL DISAPPEARING THROUGH DOORWAY
MISSING SECTION WHERE SOMETHING HAS STUCK TO PHOTO
MUG STAIN
DIM REFLECTION OF FIGURE IN KETTLE

GAMES

SUITABLE FOR CHURCH PARTIES

MUSICAL PRAYERS

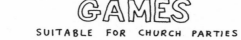

ONE KNEELER IS TAKEN AWAY EACH TIME

PASS THE COLLECTION PLATE

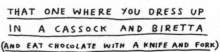

SOME MONEY MUST BE PUT IN WHEN MUSIC STOPS

PIN THE STOLE ON THE VICAR

THAT ONE WHERE YOU DRESS UP IN A CASSOCK AND BIRETTA

(AND EAT CHOCOLATE WITH A KNIFE AND FORK)

THE DISCERNMENT PROCESS

HOW TO BE SELECTED AS A MEMBER OF THE CLERGY

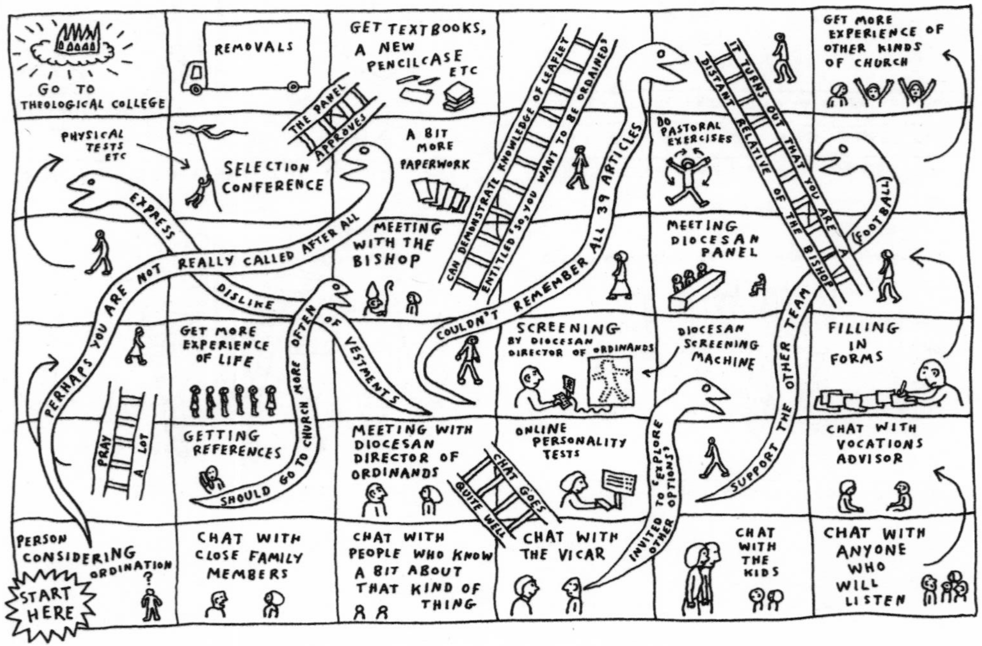

ORDINATION

THE ORDINANDS HAVE TOILED AT THEIR BOOKS FOR MANY YEARS

THEY HAVE PREPARED THEIR RECENTLY PURCHASED VESTMENTS

THEY HAVE RECEIVED A BLESSING FROM THE BISHOP

NOW, AT LAST, THEY ARE FULLY QUALIFIED TO SERVE THE CHURCH

THE CLERGY DESK

THE TRIED AND TESTED WAY TO ARRANGE IT

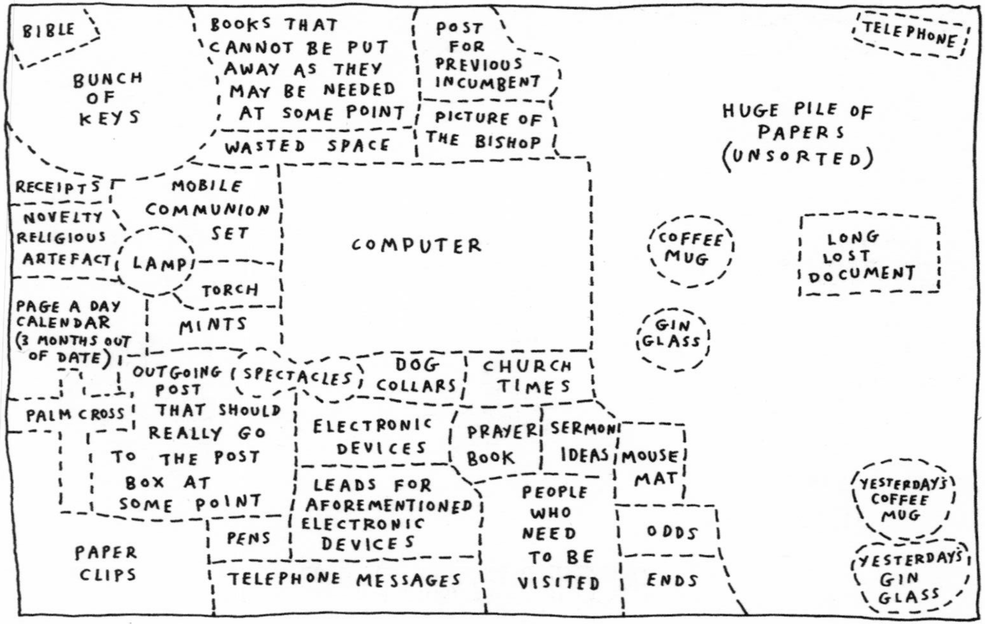

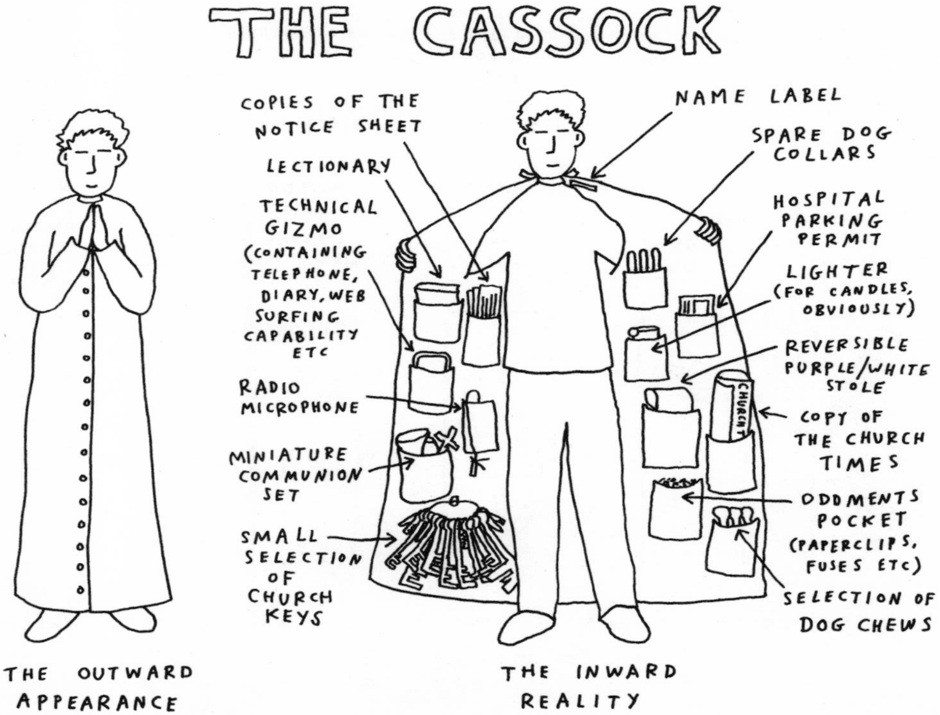
THE CASSOCK
THE OUTWARD APPEARANCE
COPIES OF THE NOTICE SHEET
LECTIONARY
TECHNICAL GIZMO (CONTAINING TELEPHONE, DIARY, WEB SURFING CAPABILITY ETC
RADIO MICROPHONE
MINIATURE COMMUNION SET
SMALL SELECTION OF CHURCH KEYS
NAME LABEL
SPARE DOG COLLARS
HOSPITAL PARKING PERMIT
LIGHTER (FOR CANDLES, OBVIOUSLY)
REVERSIBLE PURPLE/WHITE STOLE
CHURCH T
COPY OF THE CHURCH TIMES
ODDMENTS POCKET (PAPERCLIPS, FUSES ETC)
SELECTION OF DOG CHEWS
THE INWARD REALITY

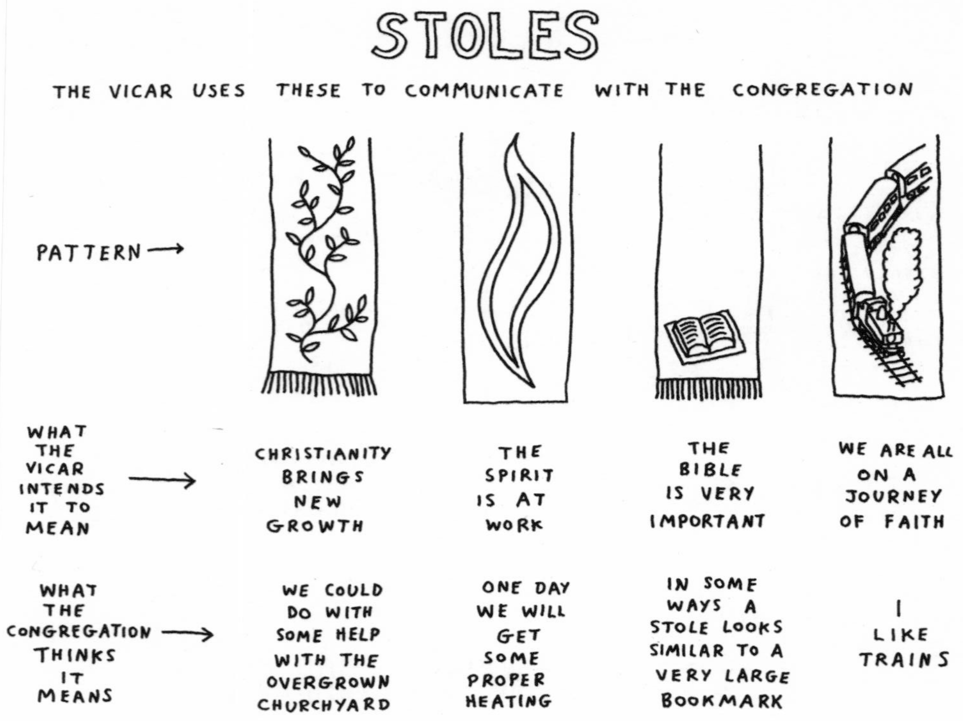
STOLES
THE VICAR USES THESE TO COMMUNICATE WITH THE CONGREGATION
PATTERN →
WHAT THE VICAR INTENDS IT TO MEAN →
CHRISTIANITY BRINGS NEW GROWTH
THE SPIRIT IS AT WORK
THE BIBLE IS VERY IMPORTANT
WE ARE ALL ON A JOURNEY OF FAITH
WHAT THE CONGREGATION THINKS IT MEANS →
WE COULD DO WITH SOME HELP WITH THE OVERGROWN CHURCHYARD
ONE DAY WE WILL GET SOME PROPER HEATING
IN SOME WAYS A STOLE LOOKS SIMILAR TO A VERY LARGE BOOKMARK
I LIKE TRAINS

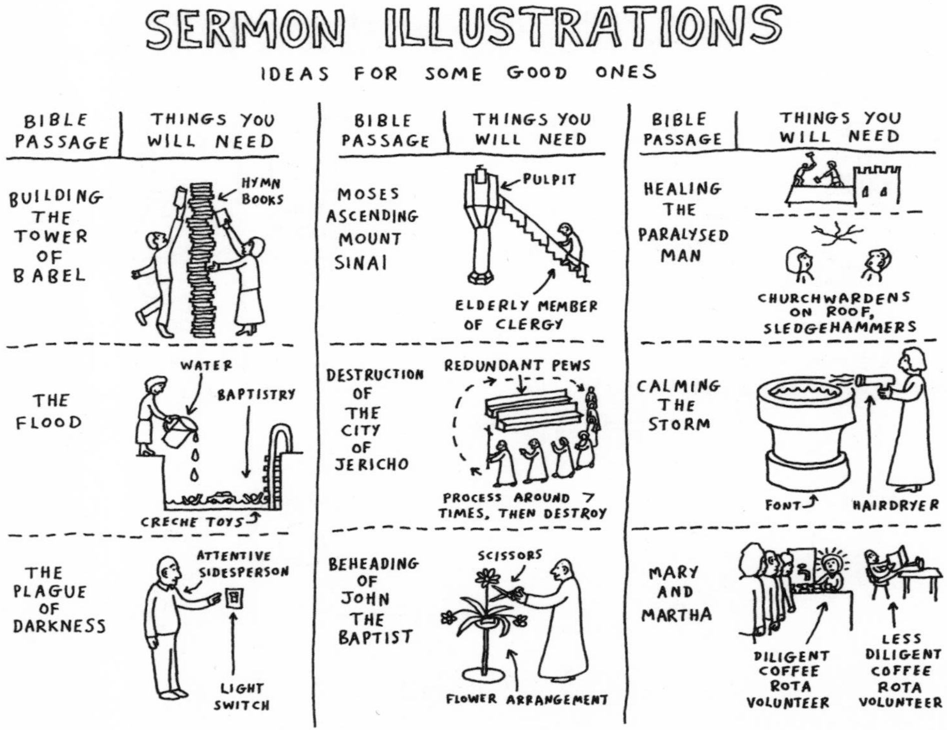

SERMON ILLUSTRATIONS

IDEAS FOR SOME GOOD ONES

BIBLE PASSAGE	THINGS YOU WILL NEED
BUILDING THE TOWER OF BABEL	HYMN BOOKS
THE FLOOD	WATER / BAPTISTRY / CRECHE TOYS
THE PLAGUE OF DARKNESS	ATTENTIVE SIDESPERSON / LIGHT SWITCH
MOSES ASCENDING MOUNT SINAI	PULPIT / ELDERLY MEMBER OF CLERGY
DESTRUCTION OF THE CITY OF JERICHO	REDUNDANT PEWS / PROCESS AROUND 7 TIMES, THEN DESTROY
BEHEADING OF JOHN THE BAPTIST	SCISSORS / FLOWER ARRANGEMENT
HEALING THE PARALYSED MAN	CHURCHWARDENS ON ROOF, SLEDGEHAMMERS
CALMING THE STORM	Font / HAIRDRYER
MARY AND MARTHA	DILIGENT COFFEE ROTA VOLUNTEER / LESS DILIGENT COFFEE ROTA VOLUNTEER

THE DAILY OFFICE
20 MINUTES
ALL OF THE CLERGY PRAY THIS EVERY DAY
40 MINUTES
IF THEY ARE TOO BUSY THEY MAKE UP FOR IT THE FOLLOWING DAY
MON
TUE
WED
THUR
FRI
5 DAYS
SOME CLERGY PREFER TO DO A YEAR'S PRAYING ALL AT ONCE
JAN
FEB
MAR
APR
MAY
JUN
6 MONTHS
OTHERS SAVE IT ALL UP AND DO ONE LONG STINT BEFORE RETIREMENT

AWKWARD PASTORAL VISITS

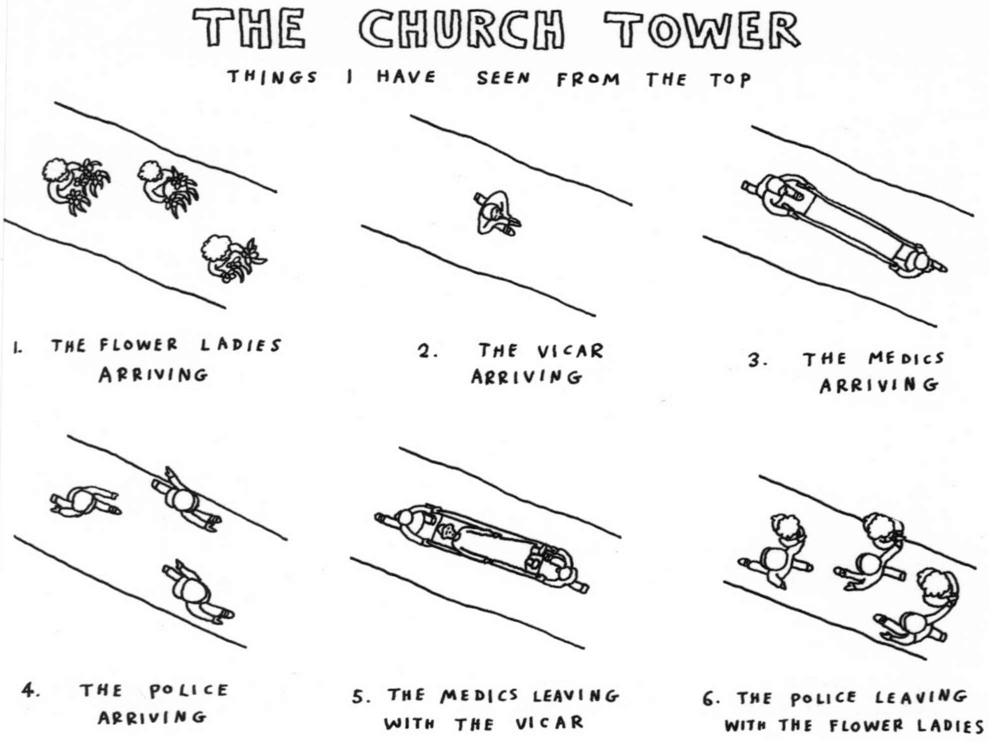
THE CHURCH TOWER
THINGS I HAVE SEEN FROM THE TOP
1. THE FLOWER LADIES ARRIVING
2. THE VICAR ARRIVING
3. THE MEDICS ARRIVING
4. THE POLICE ARRIVING
5. THE MEDICS LEAVING WITH THE VICAR
6. THE POLICE LEAVING WITH THE FLOWER LADIES

DIFFERING HEIGHTS

HOW TO COPE IN A PARISH SITUATION

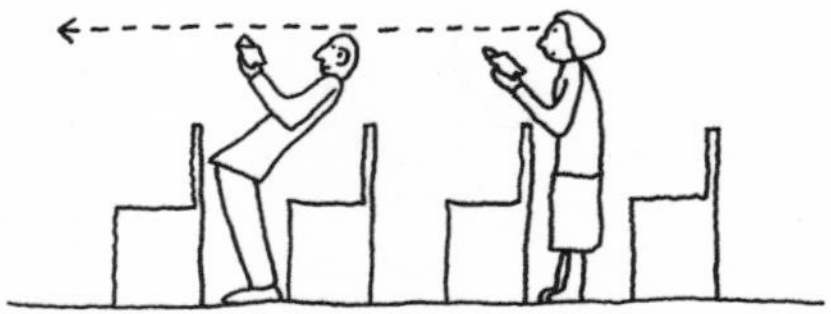

CONSIDERATE LEANING

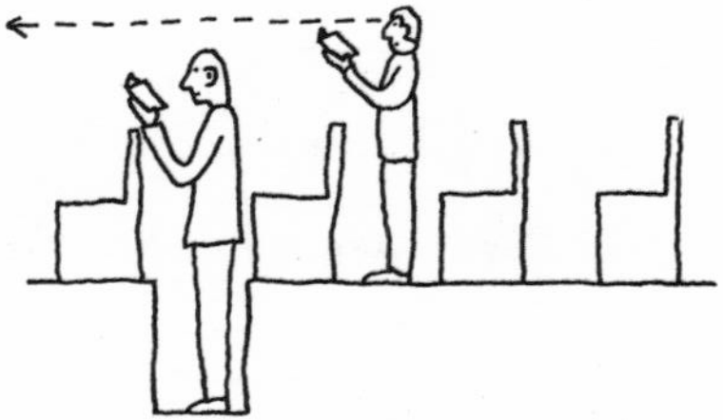

PITS FOR THE LESS SHORT

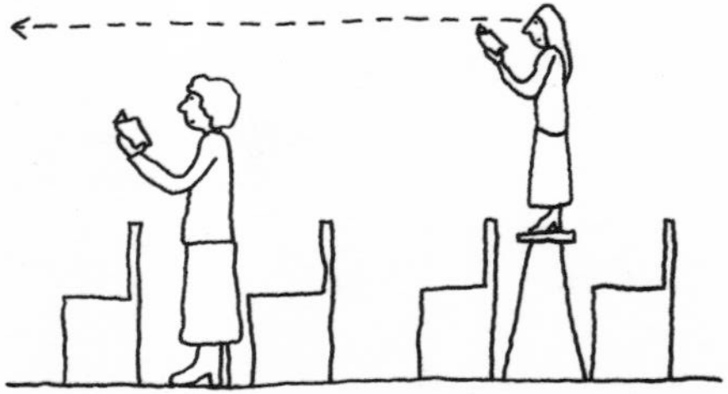

PEDESTALS FOR THE LESS TALL

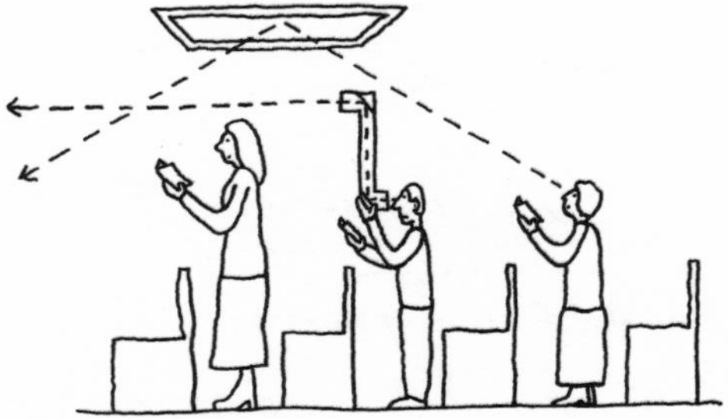

PERISCOPES AND CEILING MIRRORS

INFESTATIONS
TELLTALE SIGN
PROBABLE INFESTATION
RECOMMENDED TREATMENT
DEPOSITS ON THE PEWS
BATS
COVER THE PEWS WITH A PROTECTIVE SHEET
CONGREGATION SWATTING WITH HYMN SHEETS, OCCASIONAL CRIES OF PAIN
WASPS
HAVE A LOOK IN THE TELEPHONE DIRECTORY FOR SOMEONE WHO CAN SORT IT OUT
WOODEN BITS OF CHURCH KEEP FALLING OFF
WOODWORM
CALL THE DIOCESAN EXPERT
CONGREGATION STARTS TO BEHAVE ODDLY
CHARISMATICS
GO BACK TO THE BCP

VALUABLES

THEY ARE MARKED WITH SPECIAL DOTS THAT WILL SHOW UP UNDER AN ULTRAVIOLET LIGHT

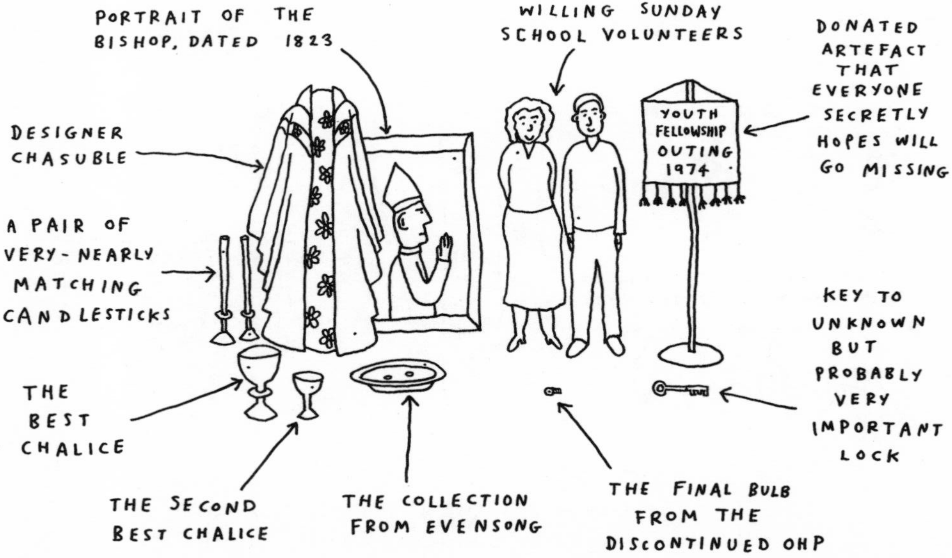
PORTRAIT OF THE BISHOP, DATED 1823
WILLING SUNDAY SCHOOL VOLUNTEERS
DONATED ARTEFACT THAT EVERYONE SECRETLY HOPES WILL GO MISSING
YOUTH FELLOWSHIP OUTING 1974
DESIGNER CHASUBLE
A PAIR OF VERY-NEARLY MATCHING CANDLESTICKS
KEY TO UNKNOWN BUT PROBABLY VERY IMPORTANT LOCK
THE BEST CHALICE
THE SECOND BEST CHALICE
THE COLLECTION FROM EVENSONG
THE FINAL BULB FROM THE DISCONTINUED OHP

THE HEATING SYSTEM

HOW TO TELL IF IT IS SET CORRECTLY

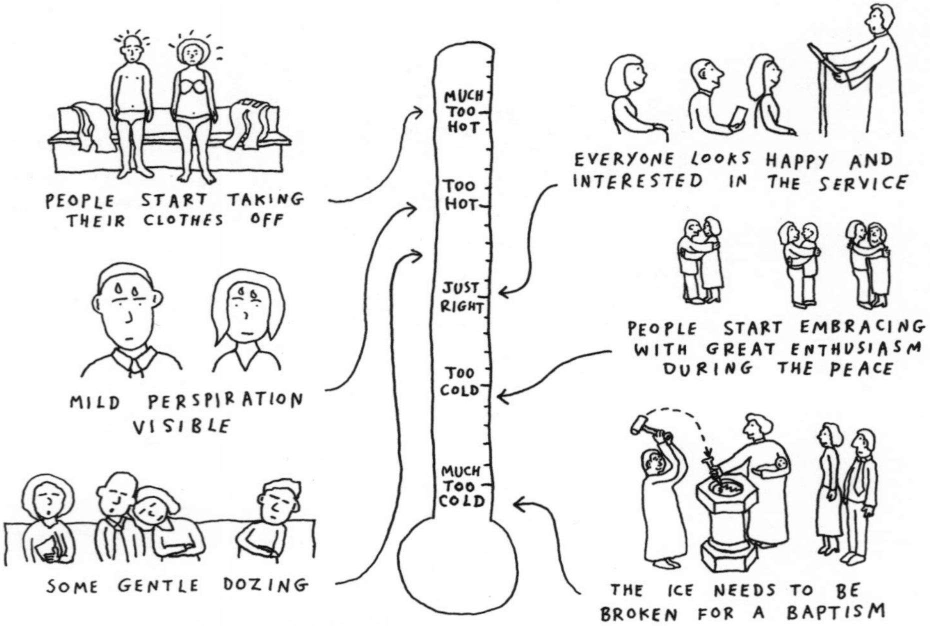
MUCH TOO HOT
TOO HOT
JUST RIGHT
TOO COLD
MUCH TOO COLD
PEOPLE START TAKING THEIR CLOTHES OFF
MILD PERSPIRATION VISIBLE
SOME GENTLE DOZING
EVERYONE LOOKS HAPPY AND INTERESTED IN THE SERVICE
PEOPLE START EMBRACING WITH GREAT ENTHUSIASM DURING THE PEACE
THE ICE NEEDS TO BE BROKEN FOR A BAPTISM

LEAD THIEVES
WE ARE WAITING ON THE ROOF SO THAT THEY DO NOT GET AWAY WITH IT
KNOWLEDGEABLE PARISHIONER READY TO DISTRACT WITH LENGTHY HISTORY OF THE CHURCH
MILITANT CHURCHGOERS
ROOF TOP PRAYER VIGIL
FLOWER LADIES PREPARE SINISTER ARRANGEMENT TO SCARE INTRUDERS
CHURCH WEBMASTER CONTINUALLY BLOGGING ALL GOINGS-ON ON THE ROOF
ROTA COORDINATOR READY TO POUNCE
SUNDAY SCHOOL MARK THE ROOF WITH GLITTER
THE CHOIR RAISE THE ALARM IN SONG

ADDITIONAL FACILITIES

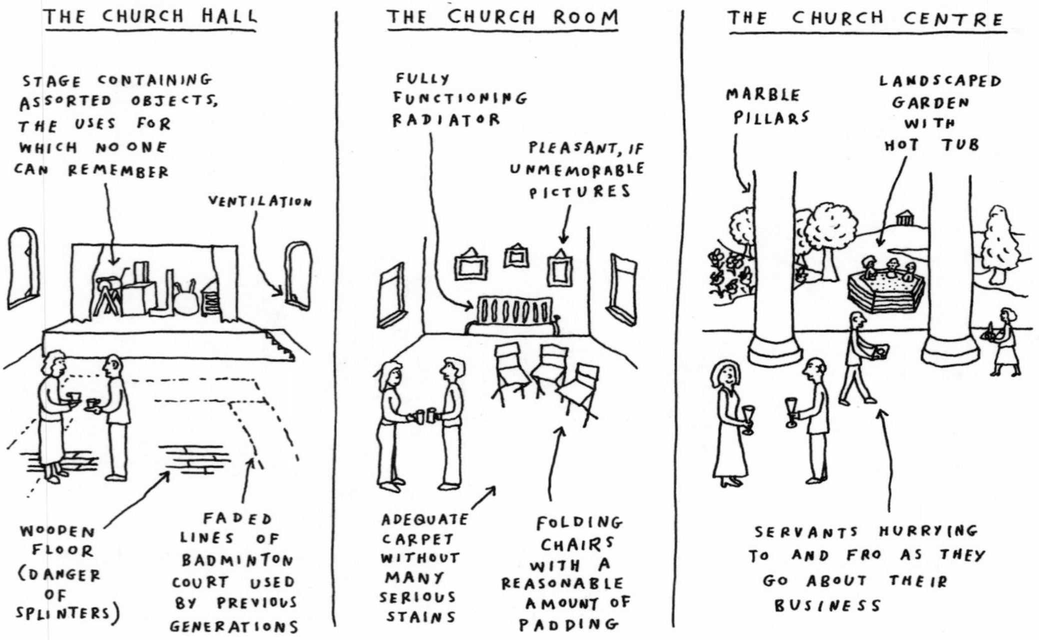
THE CHURCH HALL
STAGE CONTAINING ASSORTED OBJECTS, THE USES FOR WHICH NO ONE CAN REMEMBER
VENTILATION
WOODEN FLOOR (DANGER OF SPLINTERS)
FADED LINES OF BADMINTON COURT USED BY PREVIOUS GENERATIONS
THE CHURCH ROOM
FULLY FUNCTIONING RADIATOR
PLEASANT, IF UNMEMORABLE PICTURES
ADEQUATE CARPET WITHOUT MANY SERIOUS STAINS
FOLDING CHAIRS WITH A REASONABLE AMOUNT OF PADDING
THE CHURCH CENTRE
MARBLE PILLARS
LANDSCAPED GARDEN WITH HOT TUB
SERVANTS HURRYING TO AND FRO AS THEY GO ABOUT THEIR BUSINESS

THE CHURCH HALL
WHY WE ARE CALLING AN EXTRAORDINARY MEETING
THE PCC MEMBERS HAVE BEEN STTTING ON THE SUNDAY SCHOOL CHAIRS
THE SCOUTS HAVE BEEN MAKING TEA IN THE COFFEE MORNING TEAPOT
THE HISTORY SOCIETY HAVE BEEN USING THE PRE-SCHOOL ART EQUIPMENT
THE DRAMA GROUP HAVE BEEN USING THE SCOUT FLAGS AS PROPS
POP
THE COFFEE MORNING ATTENDERS HAVE BEEN PILFERING FROM THE YOUTH GROUP TUCK CONTAINERS
THE CHILDREN FROM THE PRE-SCHOOL HAVE BEEN SITTING ON THE DRAMA GROUP MUG SHELF
THE LADIES GROUP HAVE BEEN PLAYING WITH THE PARENT & TODDLER TOYS
THE YOGA GROUP HAVE BEEN USING THE BROWNIES' TOADSTOOL
THE YOUTH GROUP HAVE BEEN BORROWING FROM THE LADIES GROUP CROCHETING BOX
THE BROWNIES HAVE BEEN DIGGING INTO THE HISTORY SOCIETY TRUNK
THE SUNDAY SCHOOL HAVE BEEN RAIDING THE SECRET PCC BISCUIT CUPBOARD
THE PARENTS & TODDLERS HAVE BEEN LEAVING STAINS ON THE YOGA GROUP MATS

PRUNING

IN THE CHURCHYARD

BEFORE

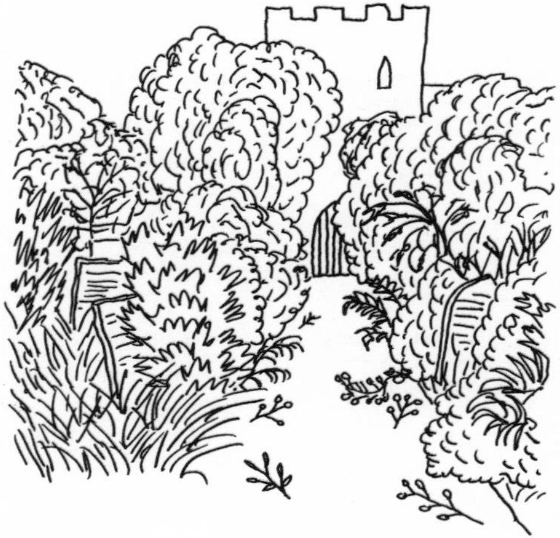

AFTER

MY SECATEURS WERE BLUNT AND MY HEART WAS NOT REALLY IN IT

HEALTH AND SAFETY

THE THINGS THAT WE ARE NOT ALLOWED TO DO ANY LONGER

HYMNBOOK HURLING

ACOLYTE FLAME-SWALLOWING COMPETITIONS

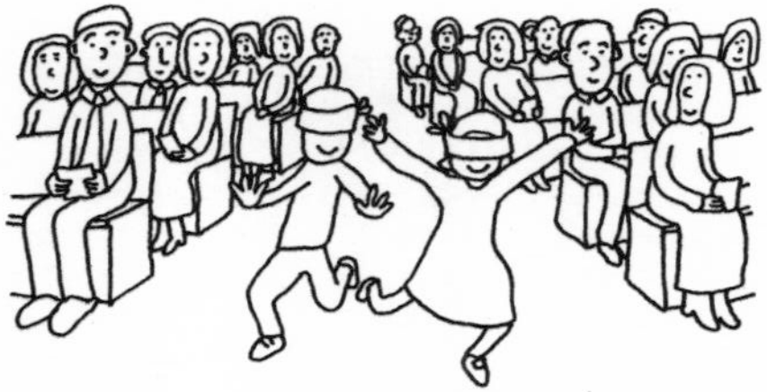

RACING BLINDFOLDED CHILDREN DOWN THE AISLE

CHANGING LIGHTBULBS USING INGENIOUS STEPLADDER COMBINATIONS

SWINE FLU

HOW TO PREVENT IT IN CHURCH

SHAKING HANDS DURING THE PEACE SHOULD BE REPLACED BY A FRIENDLY WAVE

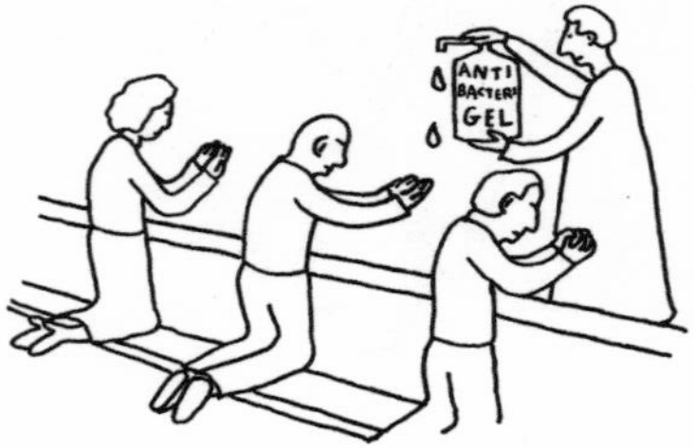

ADMINISTRATION OF ANTI-BACTERIAL GEL SHOULD TAKE PLACE

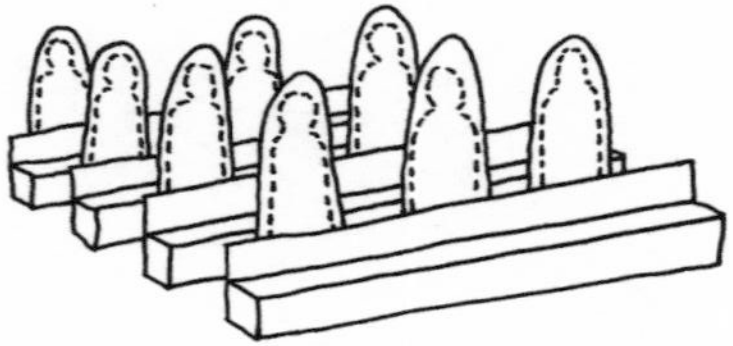

CHURCH AUTHORITIES HAVE STOCKPILED INDIVIDUAL COCOONS IN CASE THINGS GET REALLY BAD

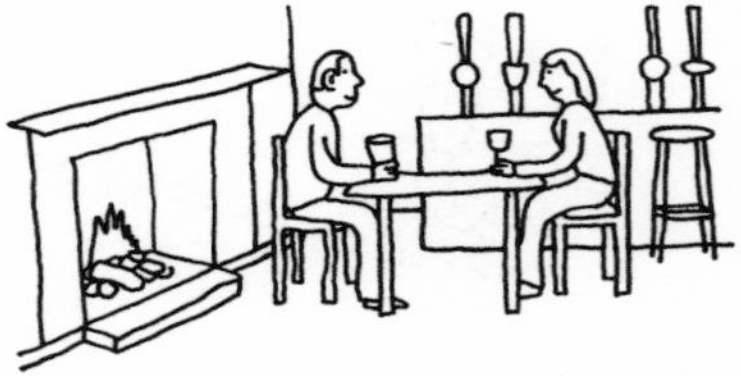

IF YOU THINK YOU MIGHT BE AFFECTED STAY IN ONE PLACE, KEEP WARM, AND DRINK PLENTY OF FLUIDS

SHARING THE PEACE

POSSIBILITIES CONSIDERED BY THE HOUSE OF BISHOPS IN THE LIGHT OF THE SWINE FLU SITUATION

THE SHEEPISH WAVE OF PEACE

THE WINK OF PEACE

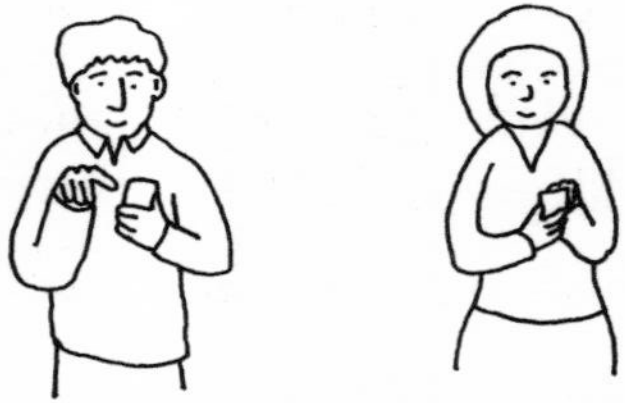

THE TEXT MESSAGE OF PEACE

ADMITTING THAT THOSE WHO DISLIKE THE PEACE WERE RIGHT AFTER ALL

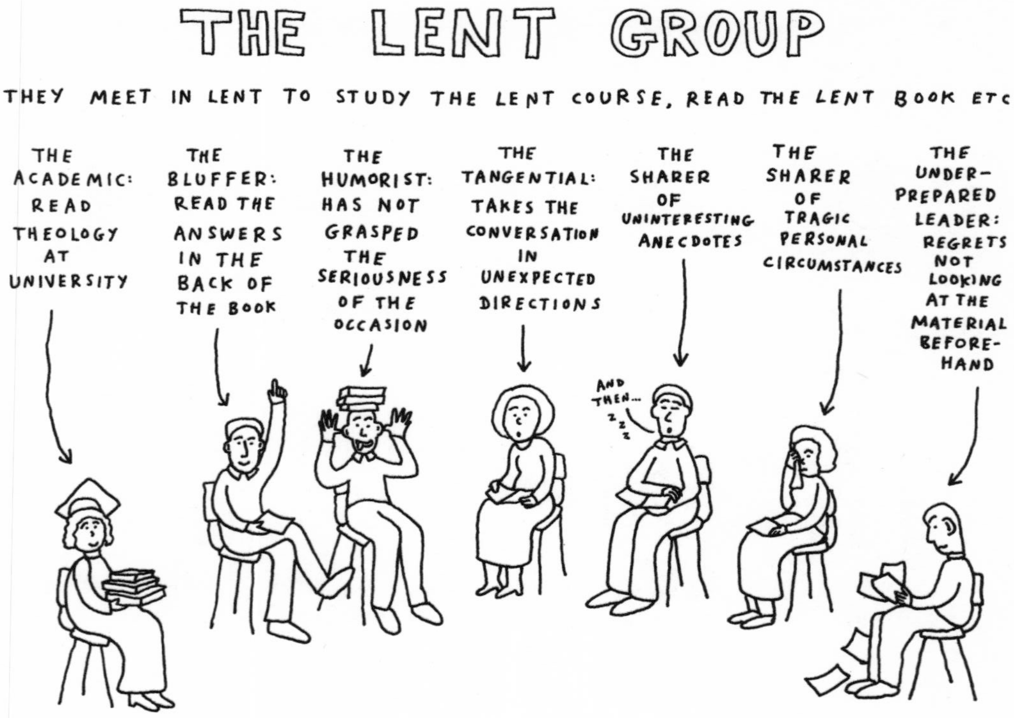
THE LENT GROUP
THEY MEET IN LENT TO STUDY THE LENT COURSE, READ THE LENT BOOK ETC
THE ACADEMIC: READ THEOLOGY AT UNIVERSITY
THE BLUFFER: READ THE ANSWERS IN THE BACK OF THE BOOK
THE HUMORIST: HAS NOT GRASPED THE SERIOUSNESS OF THE OCCASION
THE TANGENTIAL: TAKES THE CONVERSATION IN UNEXPECTED DIRECTIONS
THE SHARER OF UNINTERESTING ANECDOTES
AND THEN...
ZZZ
THE SHARER OF TRAGIC PERSONAL CIRCUMSTANCES
THE UNDER-PREPARED LEADER: REGRETS NOT LOOKING AT THE MATERIAL BEFORE-HAND

FATHER'S DAY

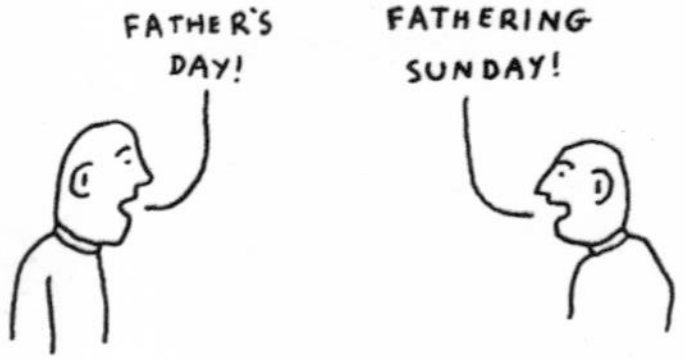
FATHER'S DAY!
FATHERING SUNDAY!

CHURCHES ARE BEGINNING TO CELEBRATE IT, ALTHOUGH THERE REMAINS SOME DEBATE AS TO THE CORRECT TERMINOLOGY

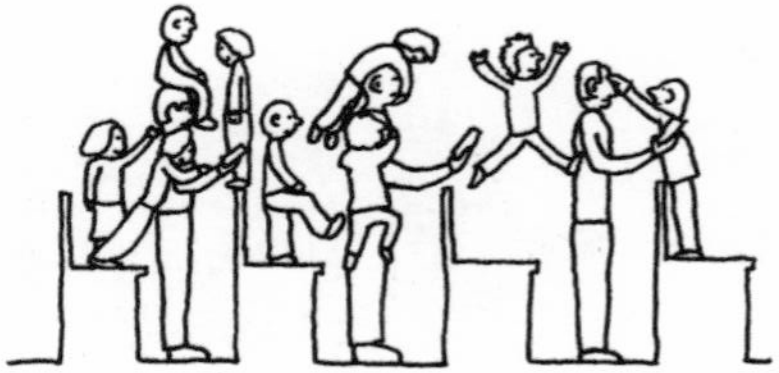

A FAMILY SERVICE IS HELD (AS FATHERS ARE KNOWN TO ESPECIALLY ENJOY THEM)

CHILDREN PRESENT THEIR FATHERS WITH A SPECIAL POSIE

ON THIS DAY FATHERS DO NOT NEED TO BE ENGAGED IN A FLURRY OF ACTIVITY. FOR ONCE THEY CAN RELAX WHILST SOMEONE ELSE COOKS THE DINNER

THE CHURCH FETE

CAKE STALL
COCONUT SHY
TOMBOLA
PLANT STALL
RECRUITMENT (ROTAS ETC)
TEAS AND COFFEES
BRIC-A-BRAC
GUESS THE WEIGHT OF THE VICAR

SUMMER HOLIDAYS

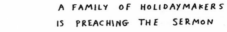

SOMEONE FROM THE DIOCESE
IS GIVING OUT THE HYMNBOOKS

A FAMILY OF HOLIDAYMAKERS
IS PREACHING THE SERMON

A RETIRED PRIEST IS
LOOKING AFTER THE CRECHE

A VISITING CHOIR IS MAKING
THE AFTER-SERVICE REFRESHMENTS

HOLIDAYMAKERS

HOW TO SPOT THEM IN CHURCH

THEY ARE DRESSED RATHER INFORMALLY

THEY ARE NOT AWARE OF THE WAY WE DO THINGS

THEY ARRIVE EARLY IN THE MORNING TO RESERVE A BACK PEW USING THEIR TOWELS

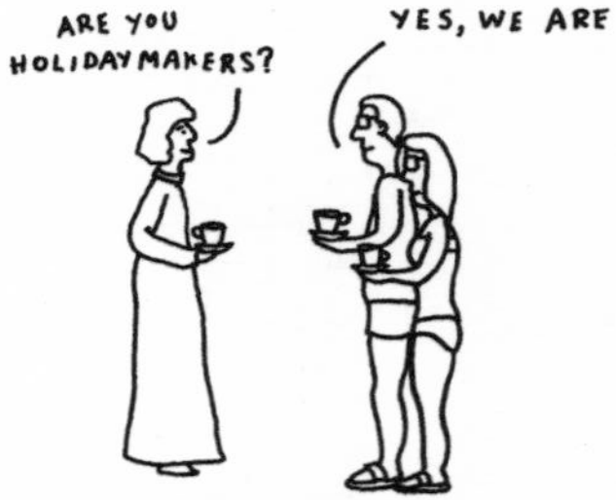
ARE YOU HOLIDAYMAKERS?
YES, WE ARE

WHEN ASKED, THEY SAY THAT THEY ARE HOLIDAYMAKERS

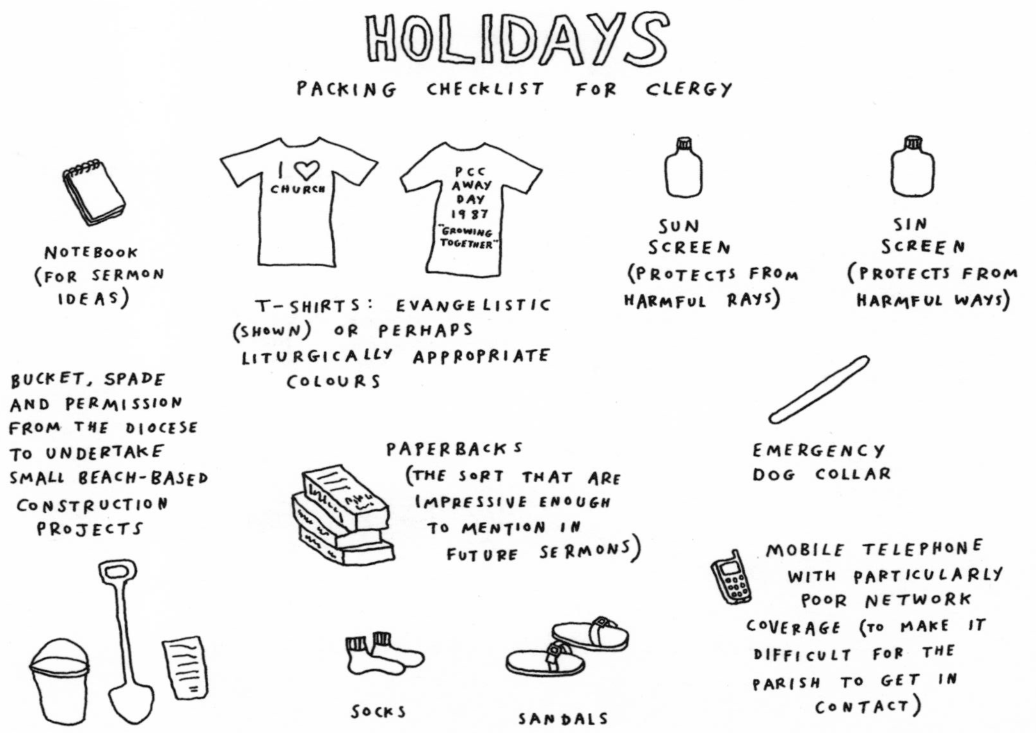
HOLIDAYS
PACKING CHECKLIST FOR CLERGY
NOTEBOOK (FOR SERMON IDEAS)
I ♡ CHURCH
PCC AWAY DAY 1987 "GROWING TOGETHER"
T-SHIRTS: EVANGELISTIC (SHOWN) OR PERHAPS LITURGICALLY APPROPRIATE COLOURS
SUN SCREEN (PROTECTS FROM HARMFUL RAYS)
SIN SCREEN (PROTECTS FROM HARMFUL WAYS)
BUCKET, SPADE AND PERMISSION FROM THE DIOCESE TO UNDERTAKE SMALL BEACH-BASED CONSTRUCTION PROJECTS
PAPERBACKS (THE SORT THAT ARE IMPRESSIVE ENOUGH TO MENTION IN FUTURE SERMONS)
EMERGENCY DOG COLLAR
MOBILE TELEPHONE WITH PARTICULARLY POOR NETWORK COVERAGE (TO MAKE IT DIFFICULT FOR THE PARISH TO GET IN CONTACT)
SOCKS
SANDALS

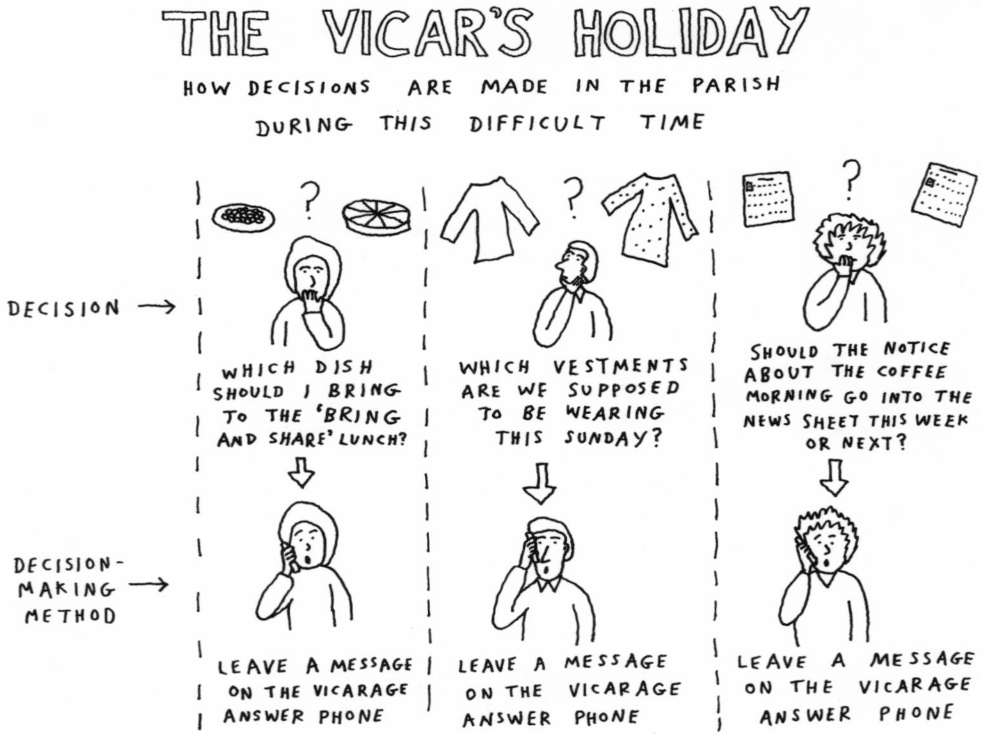
THE VICAR'S HOLIDAY
HOW DECISIONS ARE MADE IN THE PARISH DURING THIS DIFFICULT TIME
DECISION →
DECISION-MAKING METHOD →
WHICH DISH SHOULD I BRING TO THE 'BRING AND SHARE' LUNCH?
LEAVE A MESSAGE ON THE VICARAGE ANSWER PHONE
WHICH VESTMENTS ARE WE SUPPOSED TO BE WEARING THIS SUNDAY?
LEAVE A MESSAGE ON THE VICARAGE ANSWER PHONE
SHOULD THE NOTICE ABOUT THE COFFEE MORNING GO INTO THE NEWS SHEET THIS WEEK OR NEXT?
LEAVE A MESSAGE ON THE VICARAGE ANSWER PHONE

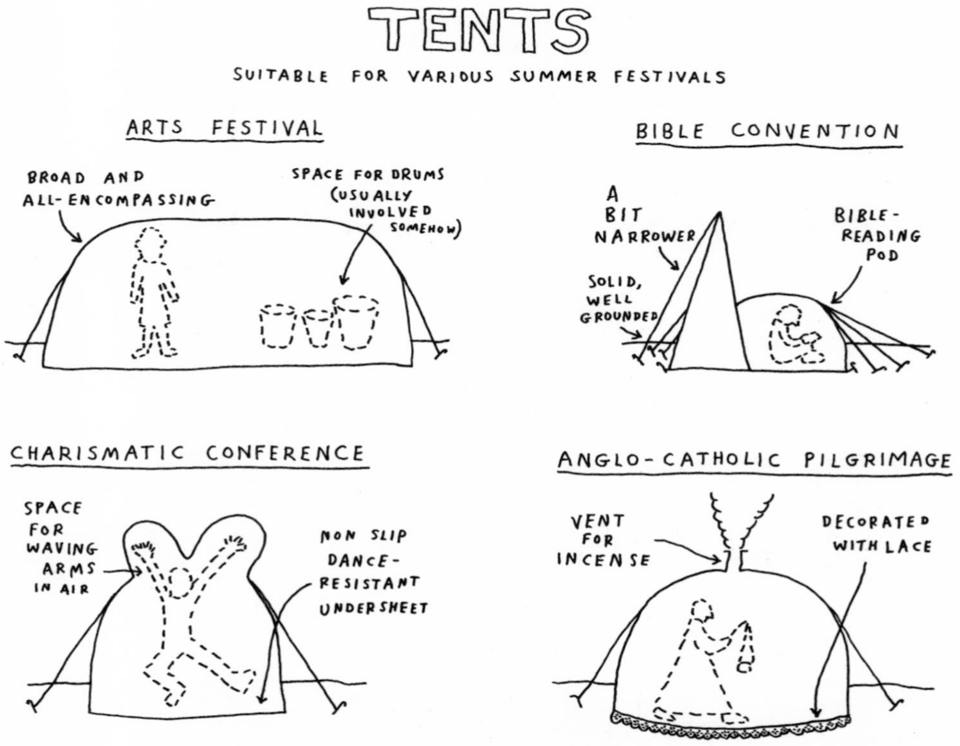
TENTS
SUITABLE FOR VARIOUS SUMMER FESTIVALS
ARTS FESTIVAL
BROAD AND ALL-ENCOMPASSING
SPACE FOR DRUMS (USUALLY INVOLVED SOMEHOW)
BIBLE CONVENTION
A BIT NARROWER
SOLID, WELL GROUNDED
BIBLE-READING POD
CHARISMATIC CONFERENCE
SPACE FOR WAVING ARMS IN AIR
NON SLIP DANCE-RESISTANT UNDERSHEET
ANGLO-CATHOLIC PILGRIMAGE
VENT FOR INCENSE
DECORATED WITH LACE

OUTDOOR ACTIVITIES

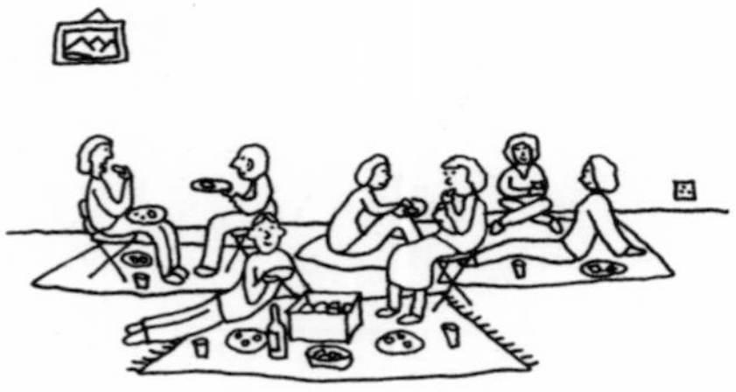

THE PARISH PICNIC*

THE BENEFICE BARBEQUE*

THE PARISH PILGRIMAGE*

THE BENEFICE BIKE RIDE*

* TO BE HELD IN THE CHURCH HALL OWING TO A CERTAIN AMOUNT OF UNCERTAINTY OVER THE WEATHER

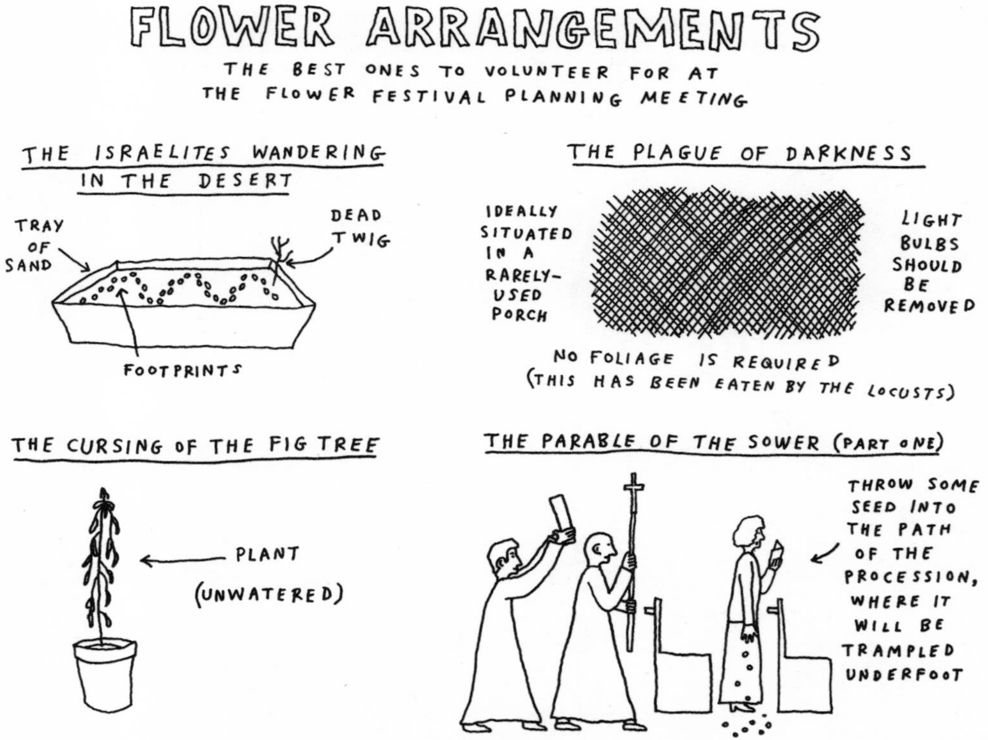
FLOWER ARRANGEMENTS
THE BEST ONES TO VOLUNTEER FOR AT THE FLOWER FESTIVAL PLANNING MEETING
THE ISRAELITES WANDERING IN THE DESERT
TRAY OF SAND
DEAD TWIG
FOOTPRINTS
THE PLAGUE OF DARKNESS
IDEALLY SITUATED IN A RARELY-USED PORCH
LIGHT BULBS SHOULD BE REMOVED
NO FOLIAGE IS REQUIRED
(THIS HAS BEEN EATEN BY THE LOCUSTS)
THE CURSING OF THE FIG TREE
PLANT
(UNWATERED)
THE PARABLE OF THE SOWER (PART ONE)
THROW SOME SEED INTO THE PATH OF THE PROCESSION, WHERE IT WILL BE TRAMPLED UNDERFOOT

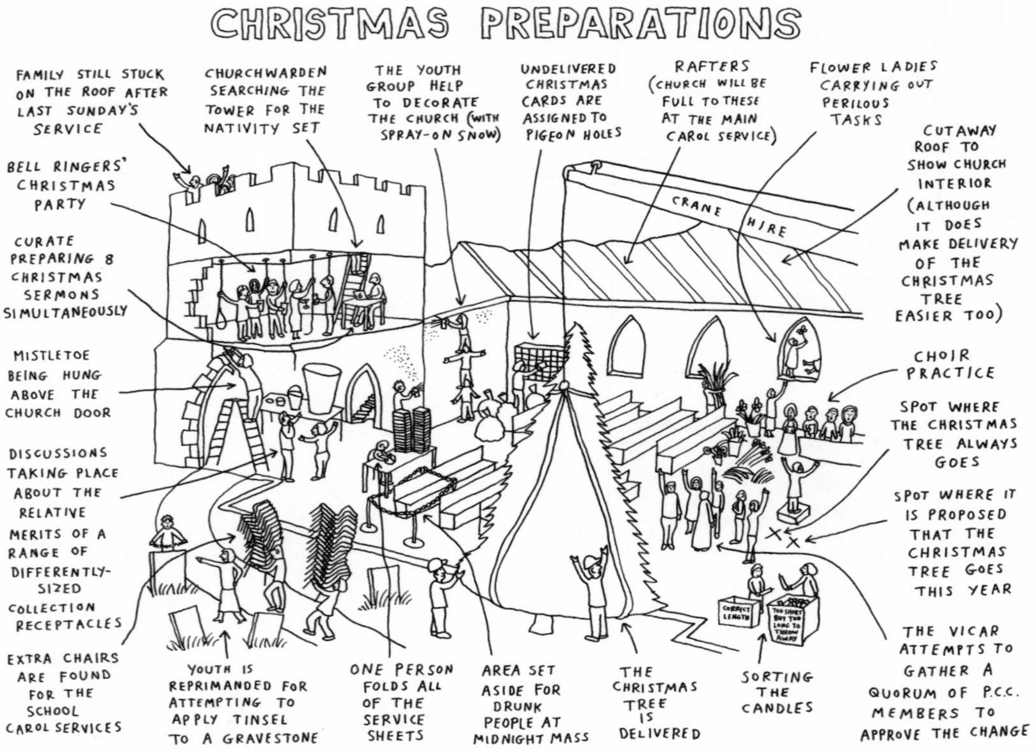
CHRISTMAS PREPARATIONS
FAMILY STILL STUCK ON THE ROOF AFTER LAST SUNDAY'S SERVICE
CHURCHWARDEN SEARCHING THE TOWER FOR THE NATIVITY SET
THE YOUTH GROUP HELP TO DECORATE THE CHURCH (WITH SPRAY-ON SNOW)
UNDELIVERED CHRISTMAS CARDS ARE ASSIGNED TO PIGEON HOLES
RAFTERS (CHURCH WILL BE FULL TO THESE AT THE MAIN CAROL SERVICE)
FLOWER LADIES CARRYING OUT PERILOUS TASKS
CUTAWAY ROOF TO SHOW CHURCH INTERIOR (ALTHOUGH IT DOES MAKE DELIVERY OF THE CHRISTMAS TREE EASIER TOO)
BELL RINGERS' CHRISTMAS PARTY
CURATE PREPARING 8 CHRISTMAS SERMONS SIMULTANEOUSLY
MISTLETOE BEING HUNG ABOVE THE CHURCH DOOR
DISCUSSIONS TAKING PLACE ABOUT THE RELATIVE MERITS OF A RANGE OF DIFFERENTLY-SIZED COLLECTION RECEPTACLES
EXTRA CHAIRS ARE FOUND FOR THE SCHOOL CAROL SERVICES
CRANE HIRE
CHOIR PRACTICE
SPOT WHERE THE CHRISTMAS TREE ALWAYS GOES
SPOT WHERE IT IS PROPOSED THAT THE CHRISTMAS TREE GOES THIS YEAR
CORRECT LENGTH
TOO SHORT BUT TOO LONG TO THROW AWAY
THE VICAR ATTEMPTS TO GATHER A QUORUM OF P.C.C. MEMBERS TO APPROVE THE CHANGE
YOUTH IS REPRIMANDED FOR ATTEMPTING TO APPLY TINSEL TO A GRAVESTONE
ONE PERSON FOLDS ALL OF THE SERVICE SHEETS
AREA SET ASIDE FOR DRUNK PEOPLE AT MIDNIGHT MASS
THE CHRISTMAS TREE IS DELIVERED
SORTING THE CANDLES

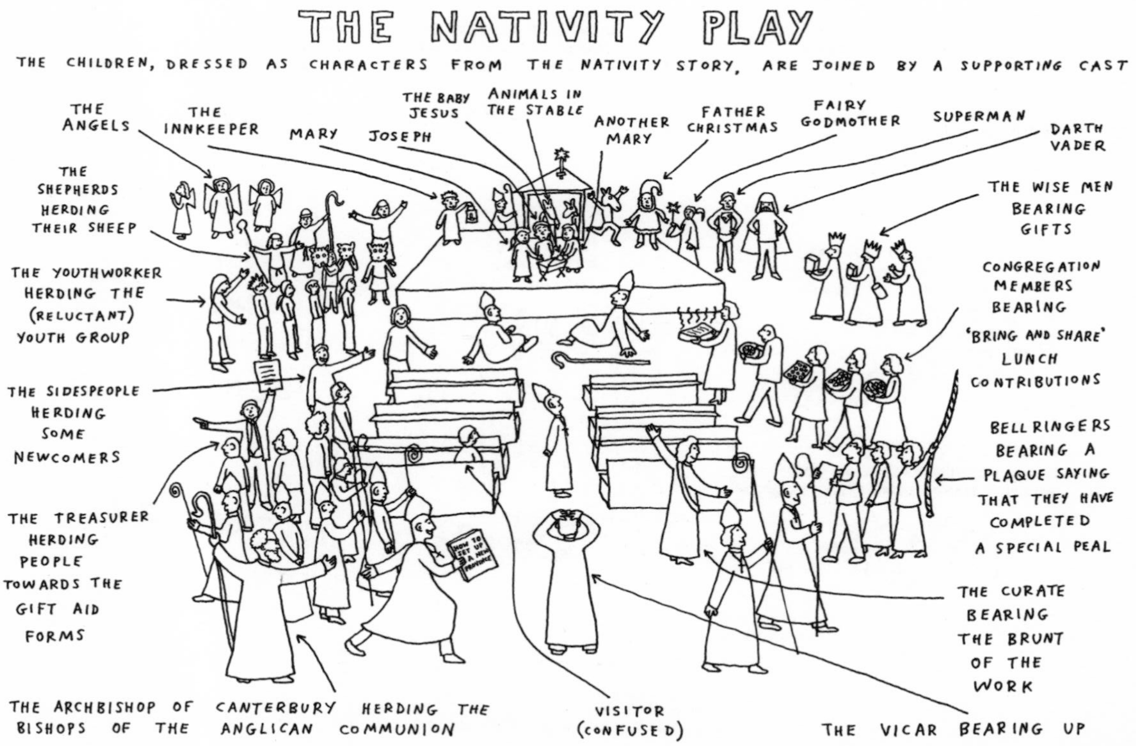
THE NATIVITY PLAY
THE CHILDREN, DRESSED AS CHARACTERS FROM THE NATIVITY STORY, ARE JOINED BY A SUPPORTING CAST
THE ANGELS
THE INNKEEPER
MARY
JOSEPH
THE BABY JESUS
ANIMALS IN THE STABLE
ANOTHER MARY
FATHER CHRISTMAS
FAIRY GODMOTHER
SUPERMAN
DARTH VADER
THE SHEPHERDS HERDING THEIR SHEEP
THE WISE MEN BEARING GIFTS
THE YOUTHWORKER HERDING THE (RELUCTANT) YOUTH GROUP
CONGREGATION MEMBERS BEARING 'BRING AND SHARE' LUNCH CONTRIBUTIONS
THE SIDESPEOPLE HERDING SOME NEWCOMERS
BELLRINGERS BEARING A PLAQUE SAYING THAT THEY HAVE COMPLETED A SPECIAL PEAL
HOW TO SET UP A NEW PROVINCE
THE TREASURER HERDING PEOPLE TOWARDS THE GIFT AID FORMS
THE CURATE BEARING THE BRUNT OF THE WORK
THE ARCHBISHOP OF CANTERBURY HERDING THE BISHOPS OF THE ANGLICAN COMMUNION
VISITOR (CONFUSED)
THE VICAR BEARING UP

NINE LESSONS
LEARNED AT THE CAROL SERVICE
①
YOU WILL NEED TO GET THERE EARLY IF YOU WANT A GOOD SEAT
②
IT'S NOT PERFECT BUT IT WILL DO
PARKING SPACES WILL BE HARD TO COME BY
③
THE WORLDWIDE CANDLE SHORTAGE HAS NOT KICKED IN YET
④
CAROL SERVICE
2008
THE SERVICE SHEET LOOKS REMARKABLY SIMILAR TO LAST YEAR'S
⑤
CAROLS WORK BEST WHEN EVERYONE HAS THE SAME WORDS
⑥
OASIS IS FLAMMABLE SO IT IS NOT A GOOD IDEA TO PUT CANDLES IN IT
⑦
SMALL CHILDREN DO NOT ESPECIALLY ENJOY LISTENING TO NINE READINGS
⑧
PARENTS DO NOT ESPECIALLY ENJOY RESTRAINING THEIR CHILDREN DURING NINE READINGS
⑨
SNEEZE
COUGH
SPLUTTER
YOU ARE HIGHLY LIKELY TO CATCH A COLD IF YOU DO NOT ALREADY HAVE ONE

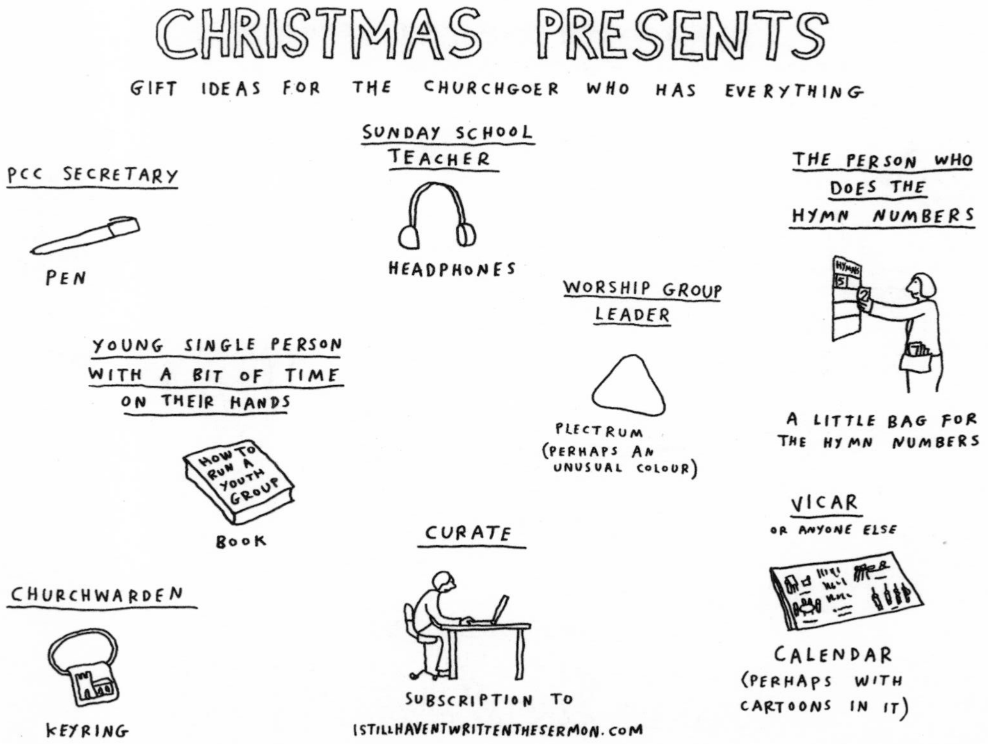
CHRISTMAS PRESENTS
GIFT IDEAS FOR THE CHURCHGOER WHO HAS EVERYTHING
PCC SECRETARY
PEN
SUNDAY SCHOOL TEACHER
HEADPHONES
THE PERSON WHO DOES THE HYMN NUMBERS
HYMNS
5
A LITTLE BAG FOR THE HYMN NUMBERS
WORSHIP GROUP LEADER
PLECTRUM (PERHAPS AN UNUSUAL COLOUR)
YOUNG SINGLE PERSON WITH A BIT OF TIME ON THEIR HANDS
HOW TO RUN A YOUTH GROUP
BOOK
VICAR
OR ANYONE ELSE
CALENDAR (PERHAPS WITH CARTOONS IN IT)
CURATE
SUBSCRIPTION TO ISTILLHAVENTWRITTENTHESERMON.COM
CHURCHWARDEN
KEYRING

NEW YEAR'S EVE

A REPORT FROM THE CHURCH PARTY

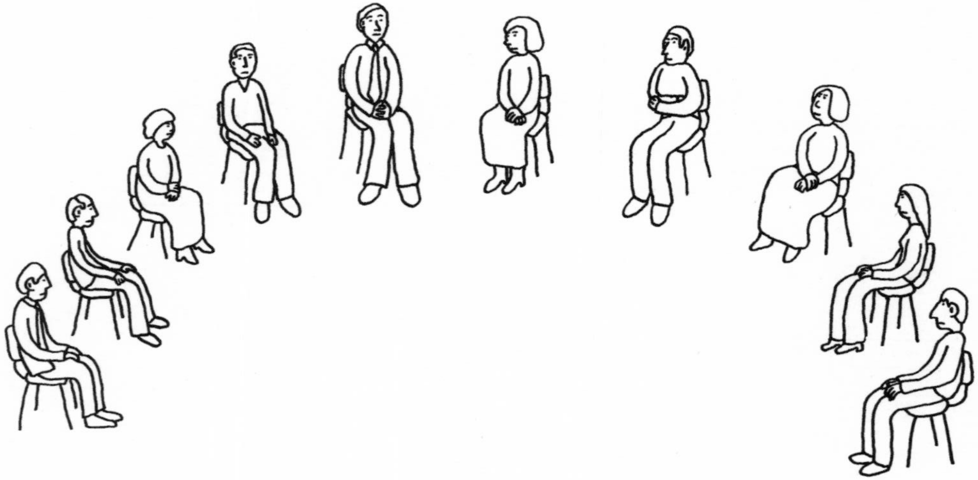

A GOOD TIME WAS HAD BY ALL

SNOW
THERE HAS BEEN SOME SNOW IN THE PARISH
ANXIOUS CHURCHGOERS HUDDLE AROUND THE RADIO HOPING TO ASCERTAIN WHETHER THE 9.30 IS GOING TO GO AHEAD
UNFORTUNATELY SOME NAUGHTY PARISHIONERS HAVE TELEPHONED THE RADIO STATION PRETENDING TO BE THE VICAR
HELLO... THERE WILL BE NO 9.30 SERVICE
THANK YOU REVEREND, WE WILL CERTAINLY BROADCAST THIS INFORMATION

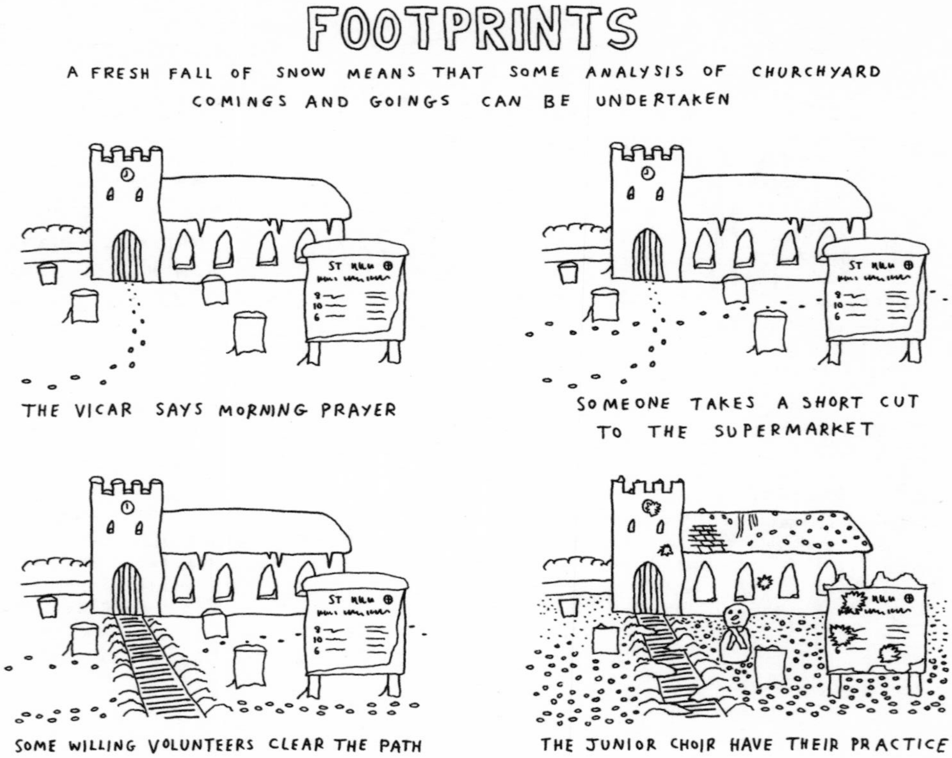
FOOTPRINTS
A FRESH FALL OF SNOW MEANS THAT SOME ANALYSIS OF CHURCHYARD COMINGS AND GOINGS CAN BE UNDERTAKEN
THE VICAR SAYS MORNING PRAYER
SOMEONE TAKES A SHORT CUT TO THE SUPERMARKET
SOME WILLING VOLUNTEERS CLEAR THE PATH
THE JUNIOR CHOIR HAVE THEIR PRACTICE

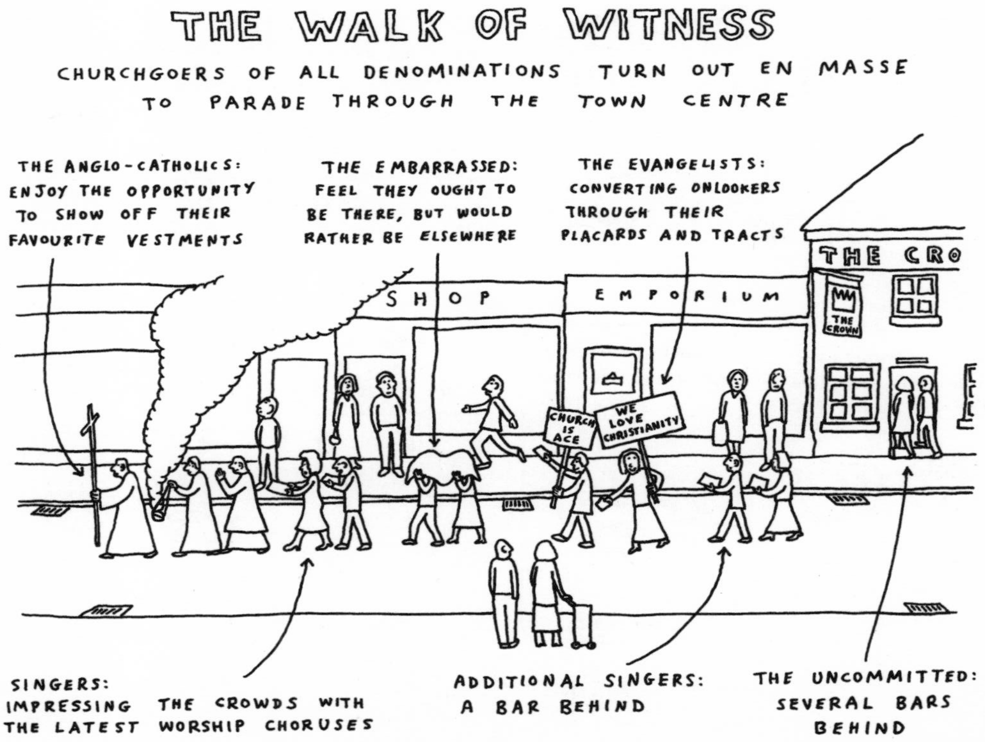
THE WALK OF WITNESS
CHURCHGOERS OF ALL DENOMINATIONS TURN OUT EN MASSE TO PARADE THROUGH THE TOWN CENTRE
THE ANGLO-CATHOLICS: ENJOY THE OPPORTUNITY TO SHOW OFF THEIR FAVOURITE VESTMENTS
THE EMBARRASSED: FEEL THEY OUGHT TO BE THERE, BUT WOULD RATHER BE ELSEWHERE
THE EVANGELISTS: CONVERTING ONLOOKERS THROUGH THEIR PLACARDS AND TRACTS
THE CRO
SHOP
EMPORIUM
THE CROWN
CHURCH IS ACE
WE LOVE CHRISTIANITY
SINGERS: IMPRESSING THE CROWDS WITH THE LATEST WORSHIP CHORUSES
ADDITIONAL SINGERS: A BAR BEHIND
THE UNCOMMITTED: SEVERAL BARS BEHIND

ECUMENISM

CHURCH 1
WE PARADE THE PATRONAL HASSOCK
CHURCH 2
WE HOP UP AND DOWN DURING THE SONGS
CHURCH 3
WE HAVE A 'TIME OF CONDEMNING' IN EACH SERVICE
CHURCH 4
WE WEAR FLORAL WREATHS (TO SYMBOLISE SOMETHING OR OTHER)
AT THE ECUMENICAL SERVICE WE PARADE THE PATRONAL HASSOCK WHILST HOPPING UP AND DOWN DURING A 'TIME OF CONDEMNING' WEARING FLORAL WREATHS (TO SYMBOLISE SOMETHING OR OTHER)

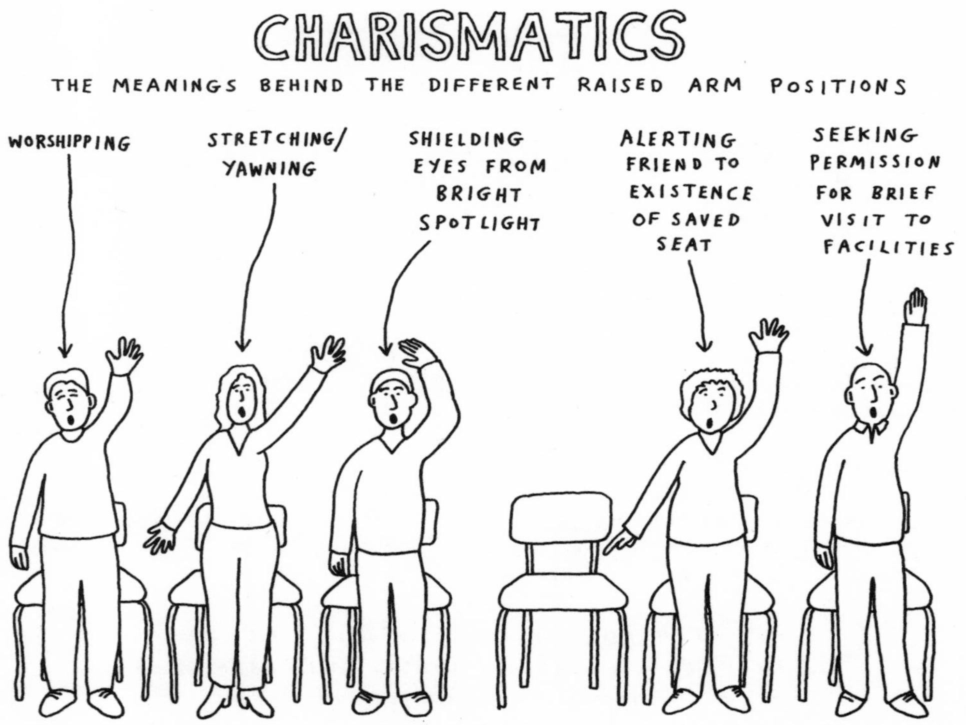
CHARISMATICS
THE MEANINGS BEHIND THE DIFFERENT RAISED ARM POSITIONS
WORSHIPPING
STRETCHING/ YAWNING
SHIELDING EYES FROM BRIGHT SPOTLIGHT
ALERTING FRIEND TO EXISTENCE OF SAVED SEAT
SEEKING PERMISSION FOR BRIEF VISIT TO FACILITIES

THE DEANERY CHAPTER

THIS IS WHEN THE CLERGY OF THE DEANERY MEET TO EAT THEIR PACKED LUNCHES

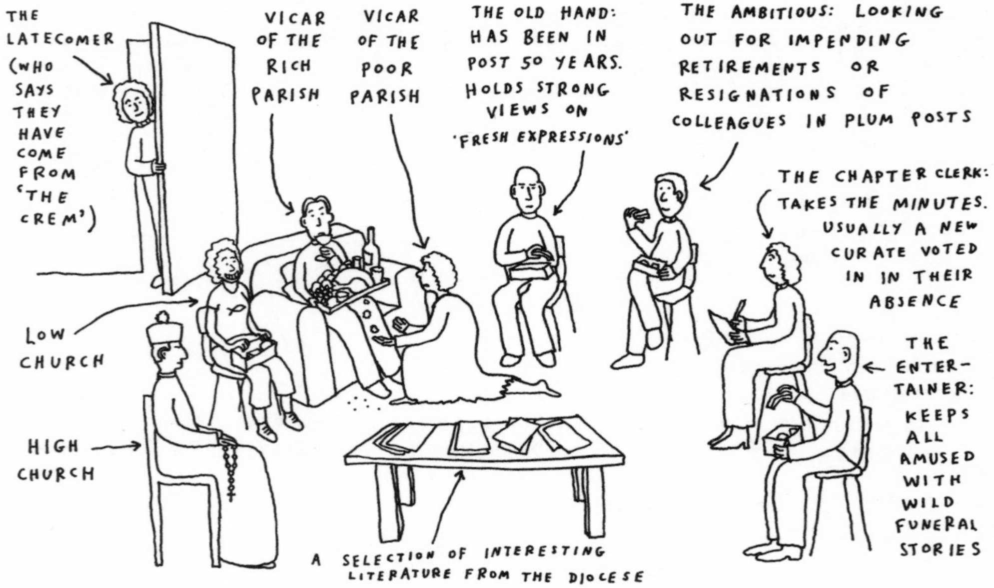
THE LATECOMER (WHO SAYS THEY HAVE COME FROM 'THE CREM')
VICAR OF THE RICH PARISH
VICAR OF THE POOR PARISH
THE OLD HAND: HAS BEEN IN POST 50 YEARS. HOLDS STRONG VIEWS ON 'FRESH EXPRESSIONS'
THE AMBITIOUS: LOOKING OUT FOR IMPENDING RETIREMENTS OR RESIGNATIONS OF COLLEAGUES IN PLUM POSTS
THE CHAPTER CLERK: TAKES THE MINUTES. USUALLY A NEW CURATE VOTED IN IN THEIR ABSENCE
LOW CHURCH
HIGH CHURCH
THE ENTERTAINER: KEEPS ALL AMUSED WITH WILD FUNERAL STORIES
A SELECTION OF INTERESTING LITERATURE FROM THE DIOCESE

ORGAN TUNING

THE ORGAN TUNER IS AT WORK IN THE CATHEDRAL

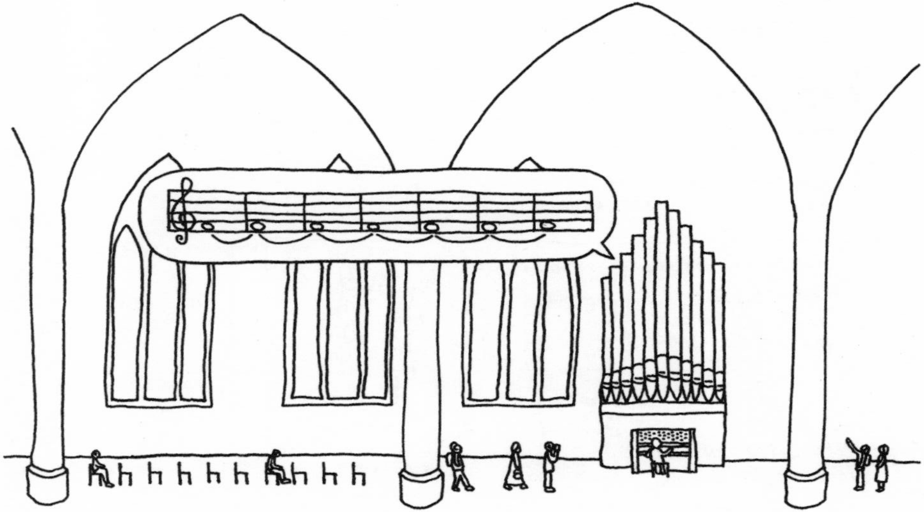

THE TOURISTS, THOUGH BAFFLED, WILL LOOK FOR THE COMPACT DISC IN THE GIFT SHOP

THE DAC

(THE DIOCESAN ADVISORY COMMITTEE)

THIS IS A GROUP OF PEOPLE WHO OFFER EXPERT ADVICE ON CHURCH BUILDINGS TO PARISHES WHO ARE THINKING OF GIVING THEM A MAKEOVER

ARCHITECT
ARCHDEACON
FIRE ESCAPE EXPERT
DOOR HANDLE ADVISOR
HANDY WITH A SEWING MACHINE
KNOWS ALL ABOUT CARPET UNDERLAY
LIVED NEXT DOOR TO A CHURCH FOR A WHILE
USUALLY FREE FOR MEETINGS ON TUESDAY EVENINGS
THE MEMBERS OF THE DAC

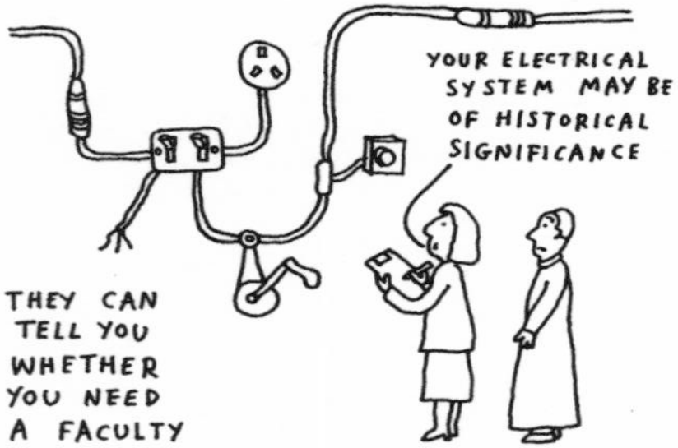
YOUR ELECTRICAL SYSTEM MAY BE OF HISTORICAL SIGNIFICANCE

THEY CAN TELL YOU WHETHER YOU NEED A FACULTY

THEY HAVE COPIES OF THE PLANS FROM PREVIOUS PROJECTS

PEWS FACING WALLS
MULTIPLE FONTS
STEEPLE AT A PECULIAR ANGLE
SWIMMING POOL IN NAVE

ESPECIALLY THOSE THAT DID NOT REALLY WORK VERY WELL

THE BISHOP'S CHAPLAIN

THEIR DUTIES ARE AS FOLLOWS:

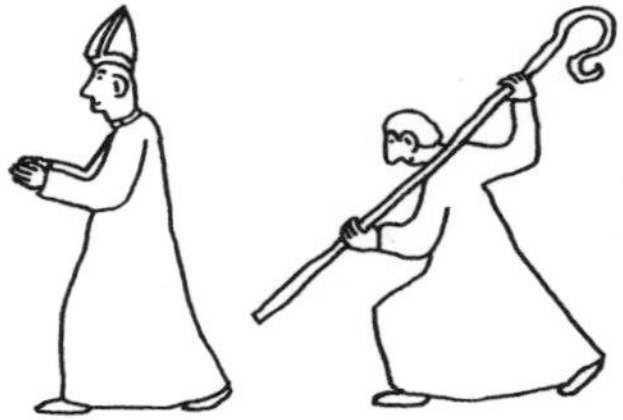

CARRYING THE BISHOP'S CROZIER AS IT CAN GET QUITE HEAVY AFTER A WHILE

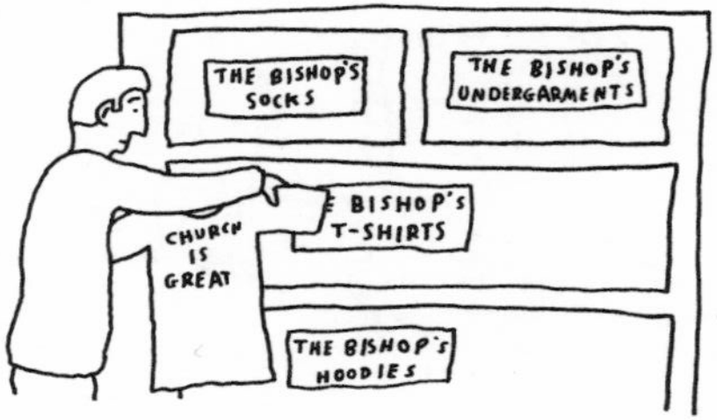

ORGANISING THINGS FOR THE BISHOP

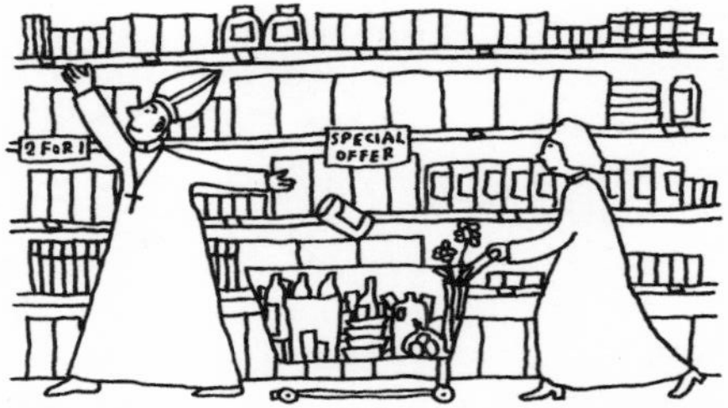

HELPING THE BISHOP TO GATHER RESOURCES

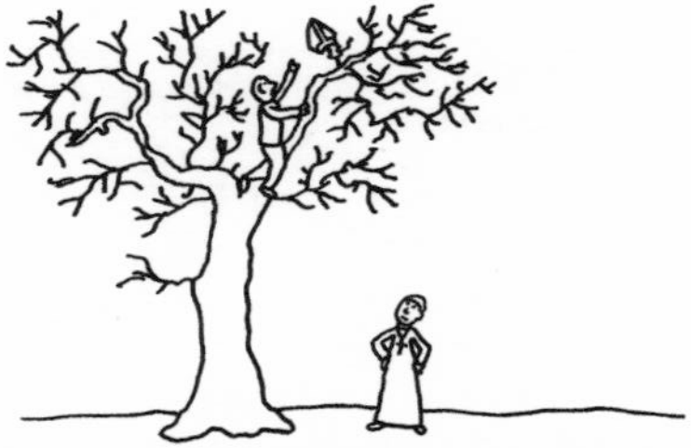

CARRYING OUT MISCELLANEOUS TASKS AS AND WHEN REQUIRED

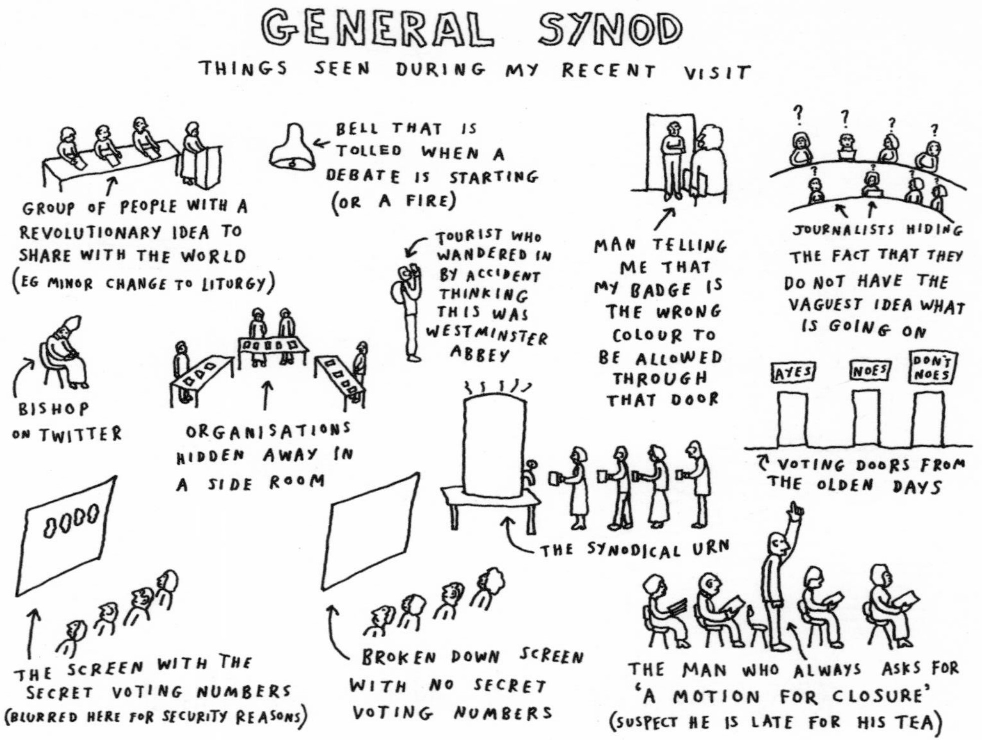
GENERAL SYNOD
THINGS SEEN DURING MY RECENT VISIT
GROUP OF PEOPLE WITH A REVOLUTIONARY IDEA TO SHARE WITH THE WORLD (EG MINOR CHANGE TO LITURGY)
BELL THAT IS TOLLED WHEN A DEBATE IS STARTING (OR A FIRE)
TOURIST WHO WANDERED IN BY ACCIDENT THINKING THIS WAS WESTMINSTER ABBEY
MAN TELLING ME THAT MY BADGE IS THE WRONG COLOUR TO BE ALLOWED THROUGH THAT DOOR
JOURNALISTS HIDING THE FACT THAT THEY DO NOT HAVE THE VAGUEST IDEA WHAT IS GOING ON
BISHOP ON TWITTER
ORGANISATIONS HIDDEN AWAY IN A SIDE ROOM
AYES
NOES
DON'T NOES
VOTING DOORS FROM THE OLDEN DAYS
THE SYNODICAL URN
THE SCREEN WITH THE SECRET VOTING NUMBERS (BLURRED HERE FOR SECURITY REASONS)
BROKEN DOWN SCREEN WITH NO SECRET VOTING NUMBERS
THE MAN WHO ALWAYS ASKS FOR 'A MOTION FOR CLOSURE' (SUSPECT HE IS LATE FOR HIS TEA)

WOMEN BISHOPS

IT IS PROPOSED THAT THEY SHOULD FUNCTION ON A REDUCED BASIS

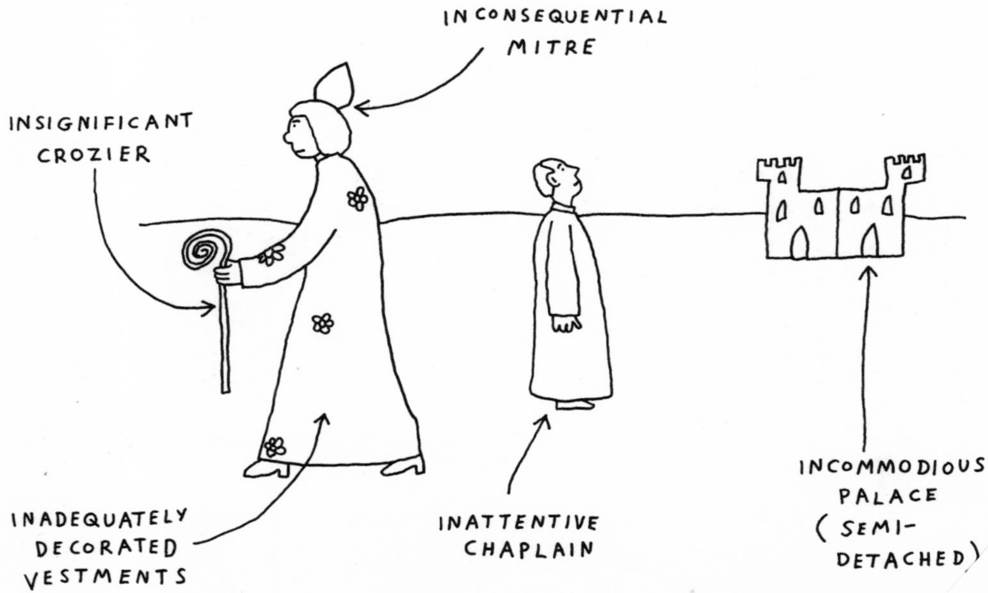
INCONSEQUENTIAL MITRE
INSIGNIFICANT CROZIER
INADEQUATELY DECORATED VESTMENTS
INATTENTIVE CHAPLAIN
INCOMMODIOUS PALACE (SEMI-DETACHED)

80

CHURCH HOUSE

A BRIEF GLIMPSE INTO THE INNER WORKINGS

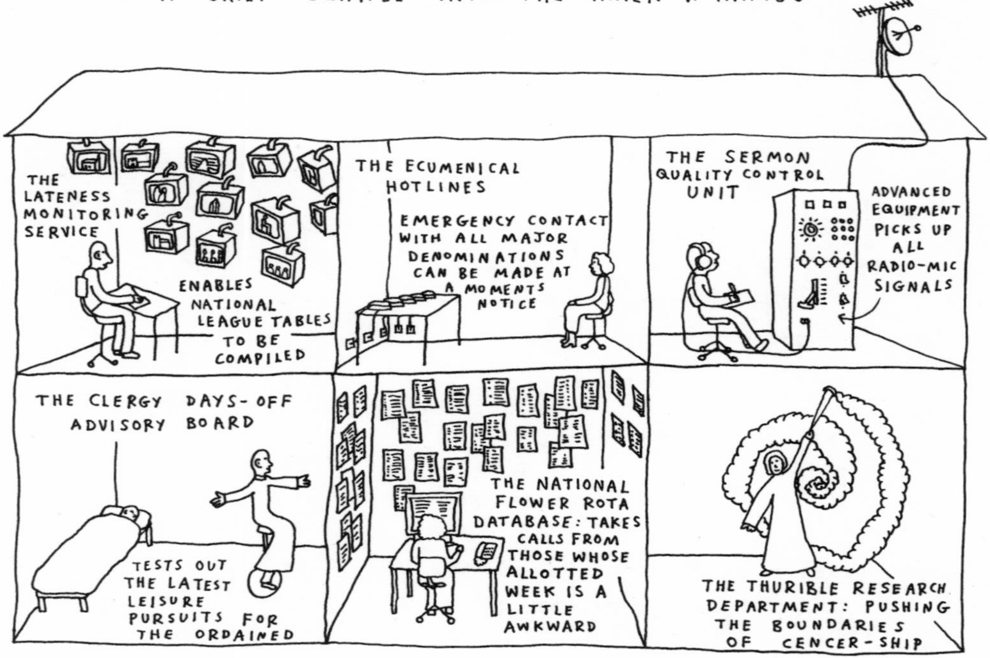

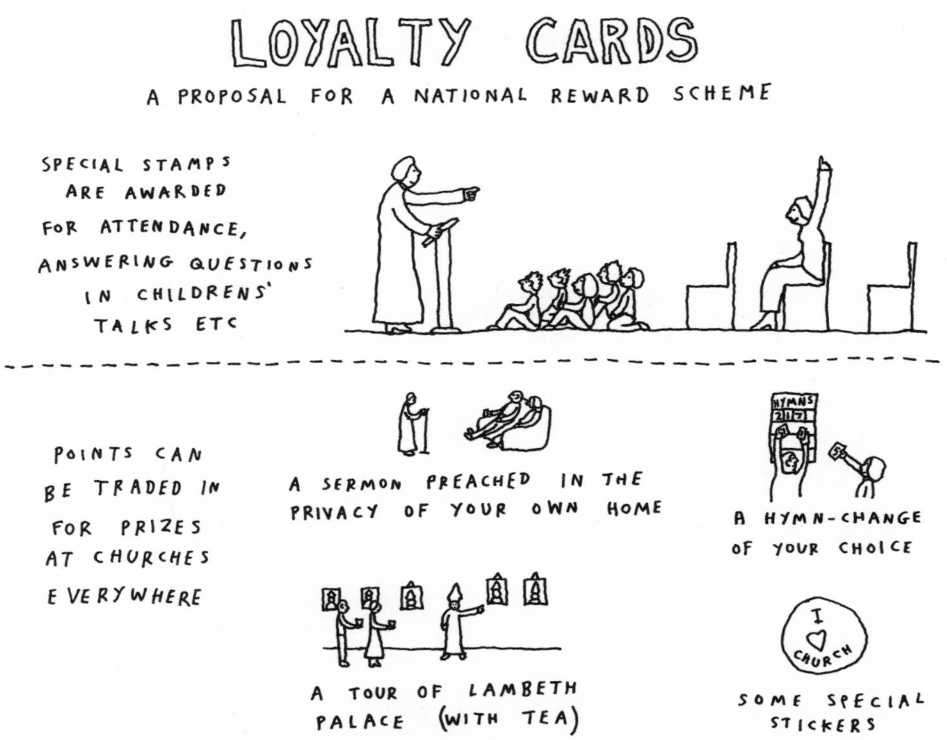
LOYALTY CARDS
A PROPOSAL FOR A NATIONAL REWARD SCHEME
SPECIAL STAMPS ARE AWARDED FOR ATTENDANCE, ANSWERING QUESTIONS IN CHILDRENS' TALKS ETC
POINTS CAN BE TRADED IN FOR PRIZES AT CHURCHES EVERYWHERE
A SERMON PREACHED IN THE PRIVACY OF YOUR OWN HOME
HYMNS
217
A HYMN-CHANGE OF YOUR CHOICE
A TOUR OF LAMBETH PALACE (WITH TEA)
I ♡ CHURCH
SOME SPECIAL STICKERS

THE SECULARISTS
LAUNCH THEIR LATEST ADVERTISING CAMPAIGN
CHRISTIANITY
DON'T CONSIDER IT
CHRISTIANITY
NOT WORTH
THINKING ABOUT
CHRISTIANITY
UNWORTHY OF
YOUR ATTENTION
CHRISTIANITY
PUT IT OUT OF YOUR MIND
CHRISTIANITY
FORGET ALL
ABOUT IT

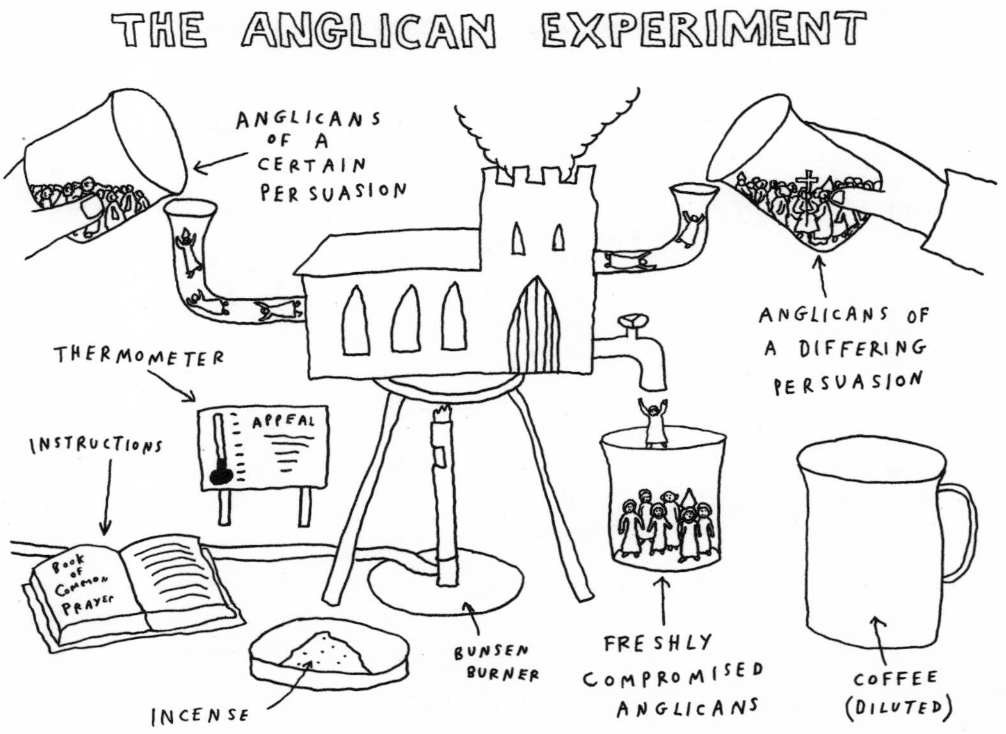
THE ANGLICAN EXPERIMENT
ANGLICANS OF A CERTAIN PERSUASION
ANGLICANS OF A DIFFERING PERSUASION
THERMOMETER
APPEAL
INSTRUCTIONS
Book of Common Prayer
INCENSE
BUNSEN BURNER
FRESHLY COMPROMISED ANGLICANS
COFFEE (DILUTED)

GAFCON

THIS IS A CONFERENCE FOR BISHOPS TAKING PLACE IN JERUSALEM THIS WEEK. IT IS NOT AN ALTERNATIVE TO THE LAMBETH CONFERENCE, BUT MANY BISHOPS ARE GOING THERE INSTEAD. THIS IS WHAT THEY SHOULD TAKE:

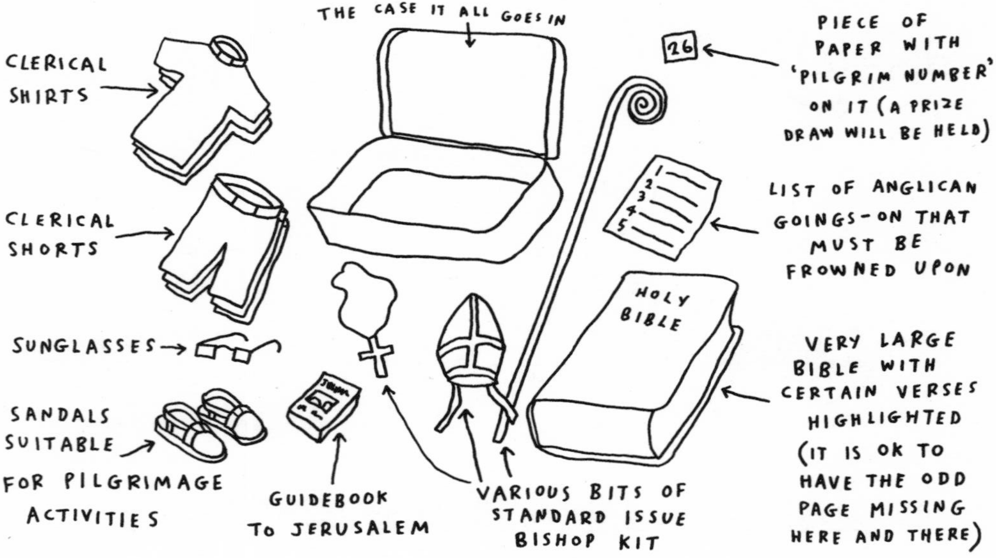

THE CASE IT ALL GOES IN
CLERICAL SHIRTS
CLERICAL SHORTS
SUNGLASSES
SANDALS SUITABLE FOR PILGRIMAGE ACTIVITIES
GUIDEBOOK TO JERUSALEM
VARIOUS BITS OF STANDARD ISSUE BISHOP KIT
26
PIECE OF PAPER WITH 'PILGRIM NUMBER' ON IT (A PRIZE DRAW WILL BE HELD)
1 2 3 4 5
LIST OF ANGLICAN GOINGS-ON THAT MUST BE FROWNED UPON
HOLY BIBLE
VERY LARGE BIBLE WITH CERTAIN VERSES HIGHLIGHTED (IT IS OK TO HAVE THE ODD PAGE MISSING HERE AND THERE)

THE BISHOPS' RETREAT

THE BISHOPS ARE HOLDING THEIR RETREAT IN THE CATHEDRAL.
I HAVE MANAGED TO CATCH A GLIMPSE OF THE PROGRAMME

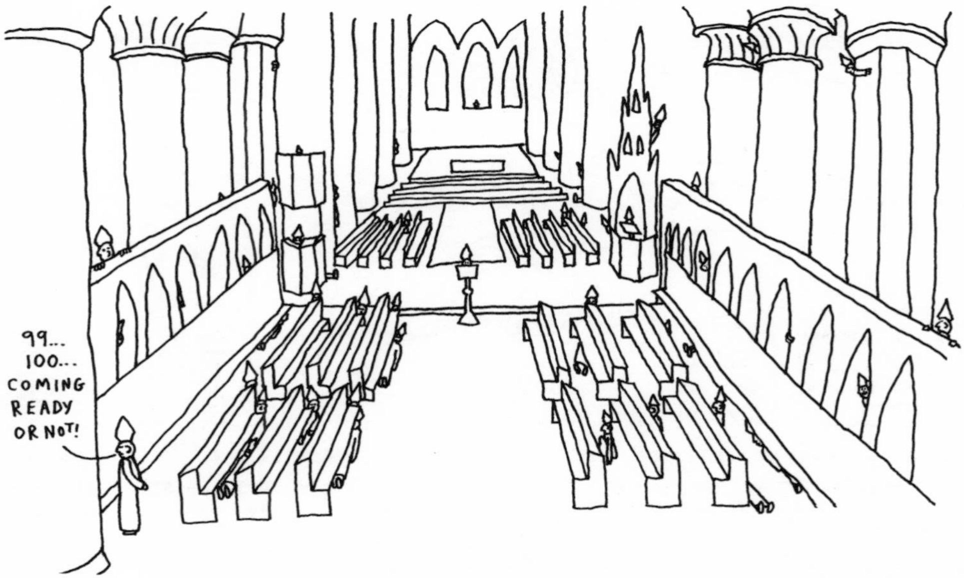

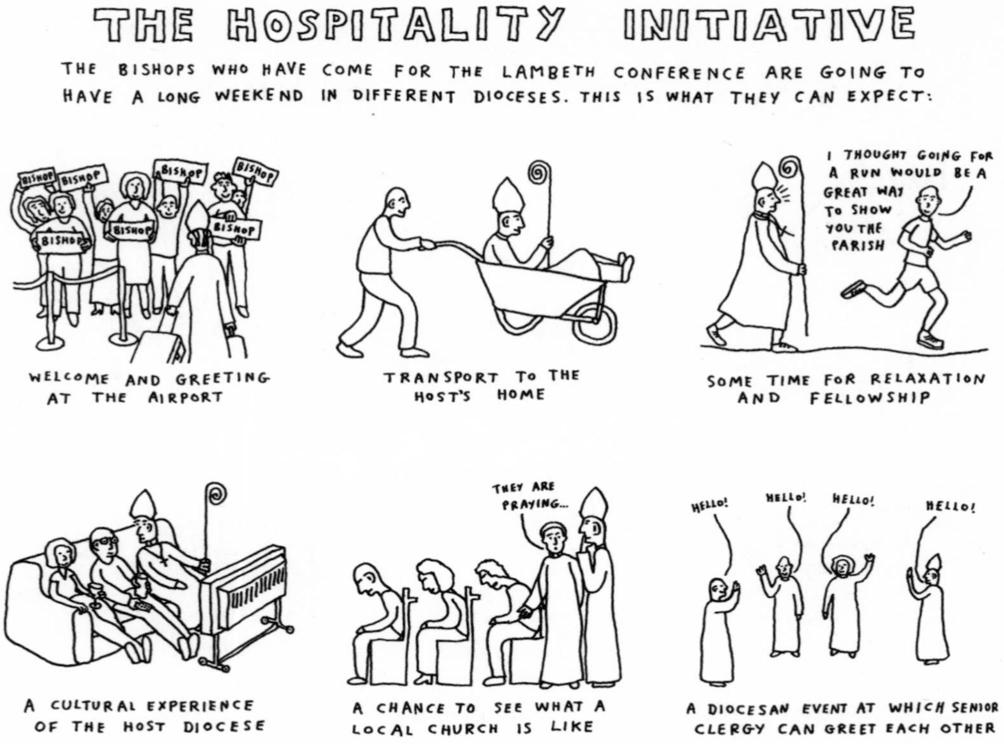
THE HOSPITALITY INITIATIVE
THE BISHOPS WHO HAVE COME FOR THE LAMBETH CONFERENCE ARE GOING TO HAVE A LONG WEEKEND IN DIFFERENT DIOCESES. THIS IS WHAT THEY CAN EXPECT:
BISHOP
BISHOP
BISHOP
BISHOP
BISHOP
BISHOP
BISHOP
BISHOP
WELCOME AND GREETING AT THE AIRPORT
TRANSPORT TO THE HOST'S HOME
I THOUGHT GOING FOR A RUN WOULD BE A GREAT WAY TO SHOW YOU THE PARISH
SOME TIME FOR RELAXATION AND FELLOWSHIP
A CULTURAL EXPERIENCE OF THE HOST DIOCESE
THEY ARE PRAYING...
A CHANCE TO SEE WHAT A LOCAL CHURCH IS LIKE
HELLO!
HELLO!
HELLO!
HELLO!
A DIOCESAN EVENT AT WHICH SENIOR CLERGY CAN GREET EACH OTHER

THE SECRET PLAN

HOW THE LAMBETH CONFERENCE DELEGATES ARE BEING ENCOURAGED TO TALK TO ONE ANOTHER

THE DEVELOPMENT OF AN ANGLICAN COVENANT

SIMPLIFIED DIAGRAM SHOWING THE PROCESS

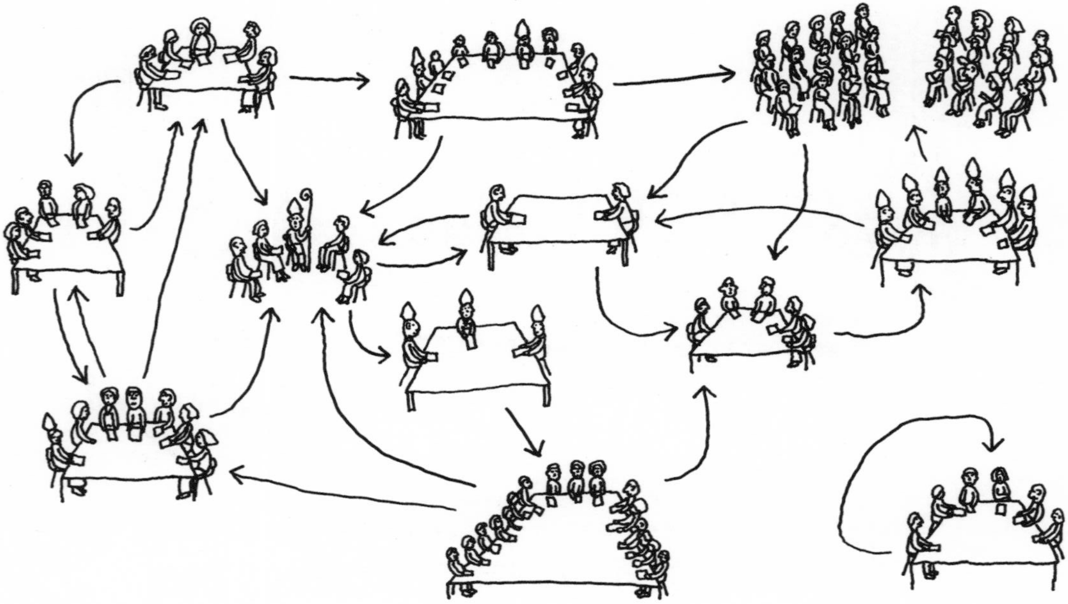

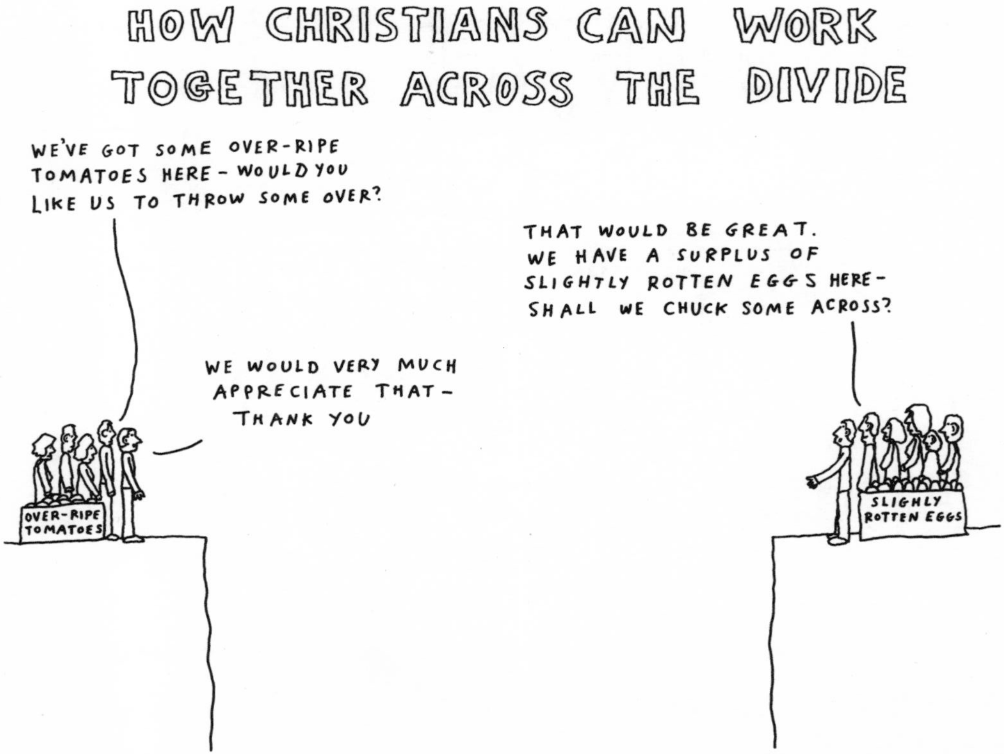
HOW CHRISTIANS CAN WORK TOGETHER ACROSS THE DIVIDE
WE'VE GOT SOME OVER-RIPE TOMATOES HERE - WOULD YOU LIKE US TO THROW SOME OVER?
THAT WOULD BE GREAT. WE HAVE A SURPLUS OF SLIGHTLY ROTTEN EGGS HERE - SHALL WE CHUCK SOME ACROSS?
WE WOULD VERY MUCH APPRECIATE THAT - THANK YOU
OVER-RIPE TOMATOES
SLIGHLY ROTTEN EGGS

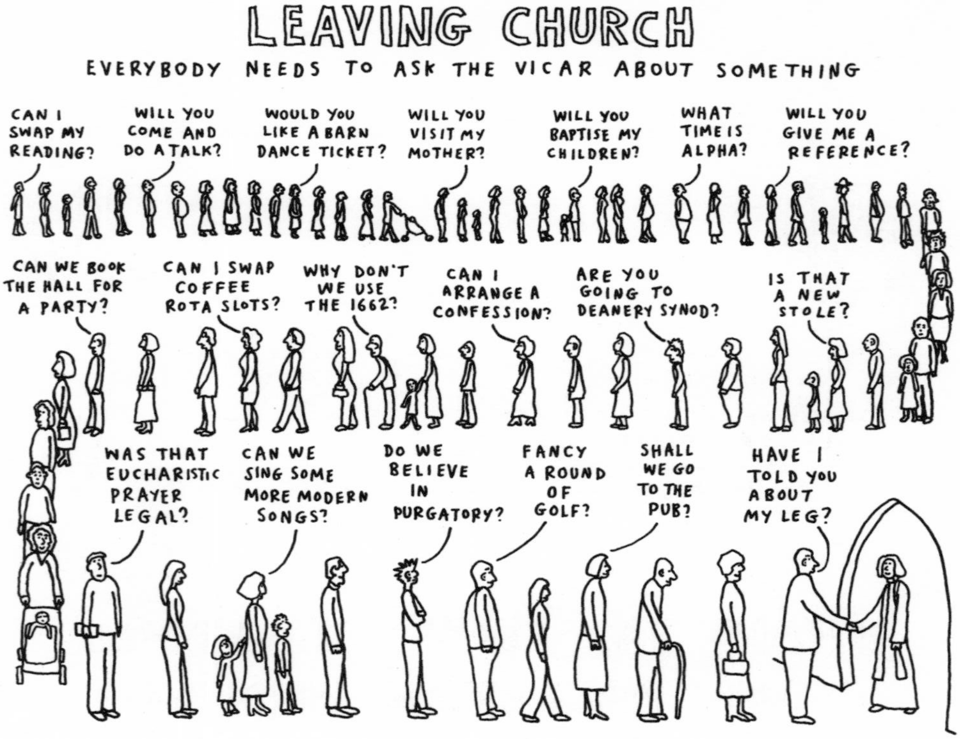
LEAVING CHURCH
EVERYBODY NEEDS TO ASK THE VICAR ABOUT SOMETHING
CAN I SWAP MY READING?
WILL YOU COME AND DO A TALK?
WOULD YOU LIKE A BARN DANCE TICKET?
WILL YOU VISIT MY MOTHER?
WILL YOU BAPTISE MY CHILDREN?
WHAT TIME IS ALPHA?
WILL YOU GIVE ME A REFERENCE?
CAN WE BOOK THE HALL FOR A PARTY?
CAN I SWAP COFFEE ROTA SLOTS?
WHY DON'T WE USE THE 1662?
CAN I ARRANGE A CONFESSION?
ARE YOU GOING TO DEANERY SYNOD?
IS THAT A NEW STOLE?
WAS THAT EUCHARISTIC PRAYER LEGAL?
CAN WE SING SOME MORE MODERN SONGS?
DO WE BELIEVE IN PURGATORY?
FANCY A ROUND OF GOLF?
SHALL WE GO TO THE PUB?
HAVE I TOLD YOU ABOUT MY LEG?